AN INTRODUCTION TO OPEN BOAT CRUISING

IAN NICOLSON
C. ENG. FRINA HON. MIIMS

AMBERLEY

Books by Ian Nicolson from Amberley Publishing

The Ian Nicolson Trilogy
Alfred Mylne: The Leading Yacht Designer 1896–1920
Yacht Designer's Notebook
Yacht Designer's Sketchbook
The Boat Improvement Guide
Build a Simple Dinghy
Boatbuilding: Cold-Moulded and Strip-Planked Wood

First published 1982, this edition published by Amberley Publishing 2016

Amberley Publishing
The Hill, Stroud
Gloucestershire, GL5 4EP

www.amberley-books.com

British Library Cataloguing in Publication Data.
A catalogue record for this book is available from the British Library.

ISBN 978 1 4456 5595 6 (print)
ISBN 978 1 4456 5596 3 (ebook)

Typeset in 10.5pt on 13pt Sabon.
Typesetting and Origination by Amberley Publishing.
Printed in the UK.

List of Suppliers and Useful Addresses

Boats

A & R Way (Phone – 07799 617534)
Character Boats (Email – enquiries@characterboats.co.uk)
Craftsman Craft (Phone – 01647 24275)
David Moss (Phone – 01254 893830)
Drascombe (Phone – 01253 896292)
Evans Boatwork (www.wbta.co.uk/evansboatwork)
FyneBoatKits (Phone – 01539 721770)
Honnor Marine (Phone – 01706 715986)
Ian B. Richardson (Phone – 01856 850321)
James Baker (Phone – 07901 002632)
John Claridge Boats (Phone – 01590 674821)
Kittiwake Boats (Phone – 01260 252157)
Lakeland Wooden Boats (Phone – 01539 727118)
Lockhart Boat Builders (Email – boats@lockhartboatbuilders.eu)
Nestaway Boats (Phone – 0800 999 2435)
Nick Smith (Phone – 07827 644223)
North Quay Marine (Phone – 01795 521711)
Ryan Kearley (Phone – 07932 458867)
Star Yachts Ltd (Phone – 07866 705181)
Willow Bay Boats (Phone – 01297 442884)

Books and Information

Adlard Coles Nautical Book Publishers (Phone – 02076 315600)
Amberley Publishers (Phone – 01453 847800)
Cruising Association (Ivory House, St Katharine Dock, London, E1 9AT)
Royal Yachting Association (RYA House, Ensign Way, Hamble, Hants, S031 4YA.
 Phone – 02380 604100)

Magazines

Practical Boat Owner (Email – pbo@timeinc.com)
Water Craft (Bridge Shop, Gweek, Cornwall, TR12 6UD. Phone – 01326 221424.
  Email – ed@watercraft-magazine.com)
Yachting Monthly (Email – yachtingmonthly@timeinc.com)

Clothing and Other Equipment

Allen Bros (Hallmark Industrial Estate, Southminster, Essex, CM0 7EH. Phone –
  01621 771689)
Holt Marine Ltd (Burnham Business Park, Springfield Road, Burnham-on-Crouch,
  CM0 8TE.
L. L. Bean Inc. (Freeport, Maine, 04033, USA. Phone: 1-800-221-4221)

Contents

CHAPTER 1

Roving Free Afloat

Early Days

On a cold cloudless night in November, I stood looking out across Southampton Water. I was on my way home from work on a Friday evening, and the weekend prospects were not exciting. It was in the early 1950s and no one went sailing in winter. Only the local ferry moved on the moonlit sea. The navigation buoys flashed, inviting everyone to get afloat. But no one would, not till the spring. I would spend Saturday and Sunday working inside the family cruiser, and maybe rub down the topsides. But it was no good starting the real fitting out. The winter frosts would ruin new paintwork.

It was that gentle night breeze which did it. I could not bear to waste it. How could anyone stand on the shore when they should be out afloat? I went back to my lodgings fomenting plans to sail in winter, all through the winter, every winter.

I was just twenty. Twenty-year-olds think of themselves as immortal. They know they are tough and self-reliant, they are sure they can deal with whatever the weather throws at them. They like the dangers of risky sailing.

Next day, instead of working on our little cruiser, I went out and searched for a cheap, tough sailing dinghy. I found one in a chaotic boatyard, lying neglected under a rotting tarpaulin. Her grey paint showed that she had been built for the navy, and I recognised the standard Admiralty shape, with full bosomy bows and broad transom. She had the low gunter rig and unbreakable steel dagger board which were standard for the class. She was clinker planked, shapely under the grime – a strongly built little beauty.

I argued with the boatyard manager over the price with all the fervour of a hard-up youngster determined to get his way. Maybe the manager thought he would never get away for lunch, maybe he was sympathetic, remembering his own eager youth. He capitulated without a prolonged battle. I started to get the boat ready at once. Thoughts of lunch melted, as I worked energetically to make the boat as seaworthy as possible.

Winter weekend sailing was fun, though often bitterly cold, partly because there were no satisfactory clothes available in those days. I learned to use waterproof industrial gloves, and made my wool hats almost waterproof by soaking them in a special compound; not much of it got onto my hair.

Weather dominated the sailing, because even my enthusiasm was tempered when squalls blasted over the water, making it impossible to launch the dinghy.

Lost weekends made me think of midweek evening sailing. That was when the most interesting sailing began.

I never dared tell anyone about it, partly because I knew it was dangerous, partly because I had an instinct that someone ... I was not sure who ... would put a stop to it.

It only worked by watching the weather: I scanned the meteorology maps daily and, as a good pattern started to develop, I made plans based on the tide. With such a small dinghy there was no sense in trying to fight the stream, even though I soon learned to work so close to the shore I navigated partly by listening to the squabbling cries of the sea-birds feeding on the tide-line.

When conditions were good, I would get afloat soon after leaving work, and slip down the river, heart pounding with the excitement of sailing in the dark, alone, in such a very small open boat. She was much too little to carry port and starboard navigation lights. I was ignorant enough to think a single torch was adequate. In practice, there was little chance of being run down. Almost all my sailing was close along the shore, sometimes too close; I spent a lot of time getting back afloat by thrusting an oar over

The Drascombe Lugger at 19 foot (5.7 metres) long, is one of the most popular open cruising boats.

the side. One night I sailed onto a submerged steel sewage outflow pipe. The clang as the metal dagger board struck caused a violent heart-snatch.

There was always the added urgency of getting back to my lodgings in time for enough sleep before dawn. When making a coastal trip to another harbour the aim was to catch the last bus or train home. But if the wind fell, or the tidal stream was too weak where I was sailing close by the shore over the shallows, I would find myself dropping behind schedule. Then it was out with the oars, to sweat, heave and slave, with anxious glances at the luminous glow of my watch every few minutes.

The bad nights were awful. Rain, blurring both sides of my glasses, made navigation difficult. If there were too many clouds it was hard to keep a check on trouble coming from squalls. The boat was so stable and the rig so low that it was unusual to get more than the occasional splash over the side, but it is hard to bail and steer at the same time.

When things did get out of hand, troubles multiplied. One moment I would be wondering if it was too early to eat the penultimate bar of chocolate (one was always kept in reserve); seconds later I was trying to decide whether to bail first, or reef, or drop the sail and plot a rough position before I got lost.

The perfect nights were moonlit, with a constant force 3 wind on the beam. With good planning, the tide would turn just when I needed it to waft me up a river to a boatyard, where I could leave the dinghy and run to the station in time to catch the train for home. The last mile sailing up the river, slipping silently between anchored fishing boats, with the moonlight so good the shore stood out clear, and the sea-birds calling, brought me back, week after week.

What added spice to a night's cruise was seeing famous yachts laid up in the boatyards. As I hurried ashore past the elegant shapes, each draped with a cover, sometimes climbing a fence to get out, or sometimes making breathless explanations to a sleepy watchman, I pitied the owners of those boats. The sight of such costly yachts, so vast and gleaming, their lovely paintwork glinting below the stars made me chortle. Their luckless owners were stuck at home, or at some dreary party, when they could have been sailing on such a night. How sad to be so wealthy as to own a massive great yacht, but be tied to a business which made it impossible to use the boat all winter.

It was true then, as it always will be, that the smaller the boat the greater the fun.

Of course, it was all thoroughly dangerous and not to be copied. I was lucky again and again, getting away with risks which must have left my guardian angel breathless. I would not recommend anyone copying this type of sailing. For a start it is nowadays so hard to get a suitable boat. An unusual combination of circumstances meant that I was exceptionally fit, and had a lot of experience in the type of boat I was sailing. The cruising ground was sheltered, the weather forecasts reliable ... and the risks quite unjustified.

Ordinary open-boat cruising is just sufficiently different to night cruising in winter. It is sensible, just dangerous enough to be fun, not so hazardous as to be senseless. It is affordable, practical, can be enjoyed almost anywhere, is ideal for weekends or longer cruises, and there are few limitations so far as age and fitness are concerned.

CHAPTER 2

The Best Type and Size of Sailing Boat

A small boat is easy to handle ashore, cheap to buy and maintain, easy to put on top of a car, and is laid up in a small space. It has all the advantages except that it is slower at sea than a big one, and it is usually less seaworthy and sea-kindly, which means it is less comfortable. It cannot carry so much gear, and it is more hampered by the weight of gear. So, like all things afloat, a compromise is needed.

Cruising boats 10 ft (3 m) long are too small, except for children, and even they are likely to have to sleep ashore. There are plenty of 12 footers (3.7 m) available and they are easy to haul out of the water, can often be carried on top of a small car, can be rowed even by an unfit crew, and they are easy enough to right after a capsize, except in rugged conditions. But they are a bit small for serious cruising and seldom large enough for sleeping aboard.

For a beginner a 14 ft (4.3 m) boat is a good compromise. It is cheap to buy, certainly secondhand, and one person can sit it out while the other cooks or navigates, provided the sail area has been modified for the wind strength. It is almost always possible to adjust the interior to enable two people to sleep aboard (see drawings) and there is enough space to carry comprehensive cruising gear for a week's voyaging.

Experienced people seem to favour the 16 ft (4.9 m) length. Astonishing journeys have been made in boats this size, partly because it is not too big to get up the beach, provided the crew of two is helped by two others properly endowed with muscle, enthusiasm and determination.

An 18 ft (5.5 m) dinghy is beginning to be a bit of a handful ashore. It needs a road trailer which is well above the basic simple minimum dinghy size. It cannot easily be turned over by two people ashore, for painting the bottom, or righted afloat after a capsize if there are adverse circumstances. It is ideal for extended cruising and is favoured by owners who are well past the beginner stage.

Open boats suitable for cruising are now available in sizes of 20 ft (6 m) and upwards, but it is not so easy to find cheap old boats above 18 ft. Ageing people who want to cruise modestly are advised to go for the biggest possible boat, and accept the fact that they are not going to be able to beach it, except at the beginning and end of the cruise. Arthritis and the other symptoms of advancing years demand a boat which is not too lively, has spare space, stays more or less upright all the time, and can carry extra comforts.

Important Considerations

When it comes to selecting the best type of boat, the principal consideration is safety. This is more important than size or comfort; it outranks speed and appearance. But it is important to buy a boat that looks good. No one should buy a boat which is not easy to love. Besides, ugly ducklings are hard to sell, and one day the boat will have to be sold to buy a bigger or faster or tougher one.

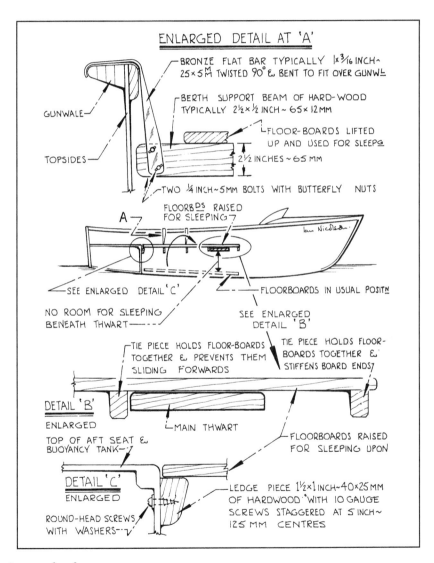

Sleeping on the thwarts
In plenty of boats there is no space for sleeping below the thwarts, so the floorboards are lifted up, and the crew sleeps on a combination of the thwarts and floorboards. Waterproof groundsheets are needed to lay on the floorboards, or some form of waterproof mattresses, such as inflatable ones, or thin closed-cell plastic foam ones.

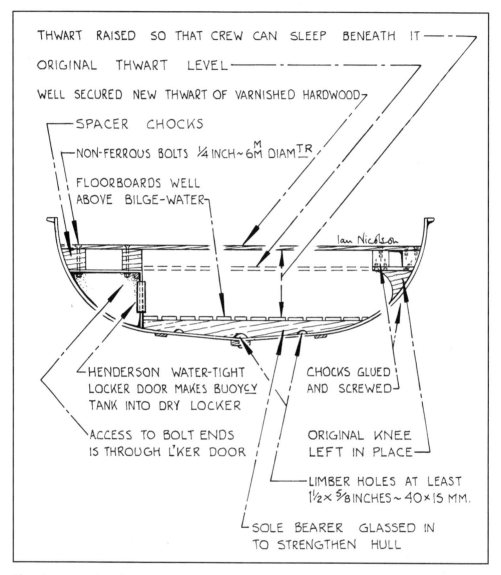

THWART RAISED SO THAT CREW CAN SLEEP BENEATH IT

ORIGINAL THWART LEVEL

WELL SECURED NEW THWART OF VARNISHED HARDWOOD

SPACER CHOCKS

NON-FERROUS BOLTS ¼ INCH ~ 6M DIAM^{TR}

FLOORBOARDS WELL ABOVE BILGE-WATER

Ian Nicolson

HENDERSON WATER-TIGHT LOCKER DOOR MAKES BUOY$\underline{CY}$ TANK INTO DRY LOCKER

ACCESS TO BOLT ENDS IS THROUGH L'KER DOOR

CHOCKS GLUED AND SCREWED

ORIGINAL KNEE LEFT IN PLACE

LIMBER HOLES AT LEAST 1½ × ⅝ INCHES ~ 40 × 15 MM.

SOLE BEARER GLASSED IN TO STRENGTHEN HULL

Sleeping space in a boat

If there is not room to sleep beneath the thwarts, it is sometimes quite easy to raise them. On the left a boat with a built-in buoyancy tank is shown, and on the right a boat with a thwart held by a pair of hanging knees. Two alternative joining techniques are detailed. On the left long bolts have been used, but before deciding on this method, try buying suitable bolts as they are not always easily found. On the right, screws with epoxy glue are used, and naturally the screws must not be the type which rust.

Safe boats tend to be beamy, with lots of freeboard and substantial scantlings. Only boats which have been designed for cruising have a bias towards safety and reliability. Typical boats are the family of craft developed round the 19 ft (5.7 m) Drascombe Lugger and its cousins, some larger, some smaller. The same firm, Honnor Marine, produce the

Explorer and the delightful Swift. The best-known cruising dinghy is the 16 ft (4.9 m) Wayfarer which has a half-sister, the 14 ft (4.3 m) Wanderer. Then there is the Laser Weekend which is 16.5 ft (5.05 m), and many others.

The place to find out about available dinghies is the advertisement section in yachting magazines. Boat shows give a good chance to compare boats, but are not necessarily the best place to buy. Indoor shows are too insulated from the weather, the salesmen can be too persuasive, and the surroundings are too far from real life afloat. It is a good idea to buy a boat outdoors on a rainy, gale-ridden day so that safety and reliability are fully in mind.

It is best to start with a boat slightly too small, especially if it is going to be necessary to haul her up beaches. Not everyone has the *élan* to go up to a complete stranger, sitting beside his car near the beach, and persuade him to back his vehicle down the beach (having first checked that the terrain is firm enough!) then get him

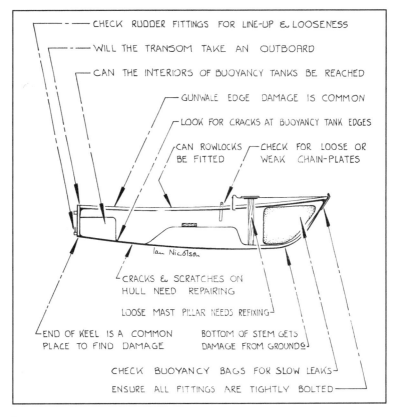

CHECK RUDDER FITTINGS FOR LINE-UP & LOOSENESS

WILL THE TRANSOM TAKE AN OUTBOARD

CAN THE INTERIORS OF BUOYANCY TANKS BE REACHED

GUNWALE EDGE DAMAGE IS COMMON

LOOK FOR CRACKS AT BUOYANCY TANK EDGES

CAN ROWLOCKS BE FITTED

CHECK FOR LOOSE OR WEAK CHAIN-PLATES

Ian Nicolson

CRACKS & SCRATCHES ON HULL NEED REPAIRING

LOOSE MAST PILLAR NEEDS REFIXING

END OF KEEL IS A COMMON PLACE TO FIND DAMAGE

BOTTOM OF STEM GETS DAMAGE FROM GROUNDS

CHECK BUOYANCY BAGS FOR SLOW LEAKS

ENSURE ALL FITTINGS ARE TIGHTLY BOLTED

Buying a boat

When going for a second-hand boat the state of the hull structure and fittings have to be examined carefully. But new boats too have many of the defects shown here because they are not always carefully moved from the building place to the sales outlet. In addition, like all mass-produced items, production problems result in poor workmanship, 'standardised' mistakes and excessive cost-cutting. A powerful flash-light is needed to look at a boat, and where possible she should be turned upside down so that the bottom can be fully examined.

to wait while a towrope is joined to the dinghy and the car. Next, this Good Samaritan has to be coaxed to drive slowly up the beach, hauling the dinghy, while the crew move the boat-rollers from the stem to the bow.

In practice, I've found it easier to recruit a large horde of children and get them to help lift or drag the boat up the beach. One needs a supply of sweets, partly to get the helpers assembled, partly to reward them once the boat is above high water. (And it is important that the boat is not dropped on one of the smaller children ... parents do object so.) All this confirms that for coastal cruising, the boat should not be too big.

For the hard-up owner, an old racing boat is tempting. It is likely to need a lot of alterations, as two of the drawings in this chapter show, but it can be a rewarding, low-cost exercise. Whatever is bought, anyone short of experience should have the boat surveyed before parting with cash.

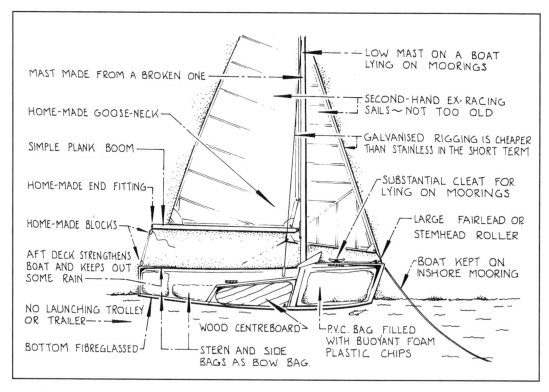

MAST MADE FROM A BROKEN ONE

HOME-MADE GOOSE-NECK

SIMPLE PLANK BOOM

HOME-MADE END FITTING

HOME-MADE BLOCKS

AFT DECK STRENGTHENS BOAT AND KEEPS OUT SOME RAIN

NO LAUNCHING TROLLEY OR TRAILER

BOTTOM FIBREGLASSED

WOOD CENTREBOARD

STERN AND SIDE BAGS AS BOW BAG.

LOW MAST ON A BOAT LYING ON MOORINGS

SECOND-HAND EX-RACING SAILS ~ NOT TOO OLD

GALVANISED RIGGING IS CHEAPER THAN STAINLESS IN THE SHORT TERM

SUBSTANTIAL CLEAT FOR LYING ON MOORINGS

LARGE FAIRLEAD OR STEMHEAD ROLLER

BOAT KEPT ON INSHORE MOORING

P.V.C. BAG FILLED WITH BUOYANT FOAM PLASTIC CHIPS

Ultra low-cost boat

Shown here are a few of the tricks which can be used to get afloat cheaply. The boat is kept on a drying or shallow mooring so no launching trolley or trailer is needed. The hull may be an old one reinforced, maybe an ex-racing boat which has lost her rig, or had it passed on to a newer boat. The buoyancy bags are home-made but must be carefully tested, as all the gear should, before voyaging far. Some old boats have metal centreboards which strain a boat considerably, so it may pay to change to a wood one, if the casing is wide enough.

Making up parts, or even spars takes time but it saves money and adds to the enjoyment of owning the boat. Building a complete boat takes skill and experience but buying a bare hull and completing it is not difficult and can save almost half the cost of a new boat.

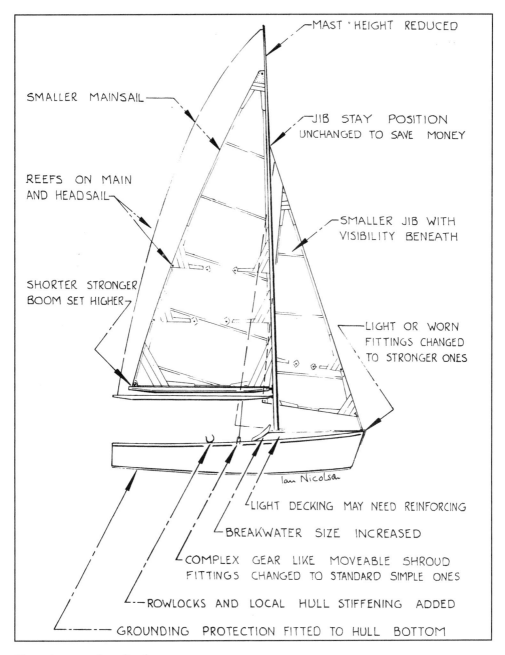

MAST HEIGHT REDUCED

SMALLER MAINSAIL

JIB STAY POSITION
UNCHANGED TO SAVE MONEY

REEFS ON MAIN
AND HEADSAIL

SMALLER JIB WITH
VISIBILITY BENEATH

SHORTER STRONGER
BOOM SET HIGHER

LIGHT OR WORN
FITTINGS CHANGED
TO STRONGER ONES

Ian Nicolson

LIGHT DECKING MAY NEED REINFORCING

BREAKWATER SIZE INCREASED

COMPLEX GEAR LIKE MOVEABLE SHROUD
FITTINGS CHANGED TO STANDARD SIMPLE ONES

ROWLOCKS AND LOCAL HULL STIFFENING ADDED

GROUNDING PROTECTION FITTED TO HULL BOTTOM

Changing a racing dinghy

A cheap cruising dinghy is a converted racing one. Shown here are just some of the jobs needed on most racing dinghies to make them suitable for cruising seriously. The weak and very light components need strengthening or changing, the sail area and height must be reduced, and the boat must be able to stand up to the rougher conditions.

It may be better to buy a new mainsail than re-cut an old one, and the same goes for the jib. But it will almost certainly be cheaper to alter the mast than to have a new one. However, it is sometimes possible to buy a racing dinghy hull without its rig, when the owner wants a new shell but wishes to hold on to his successful sails and spars.

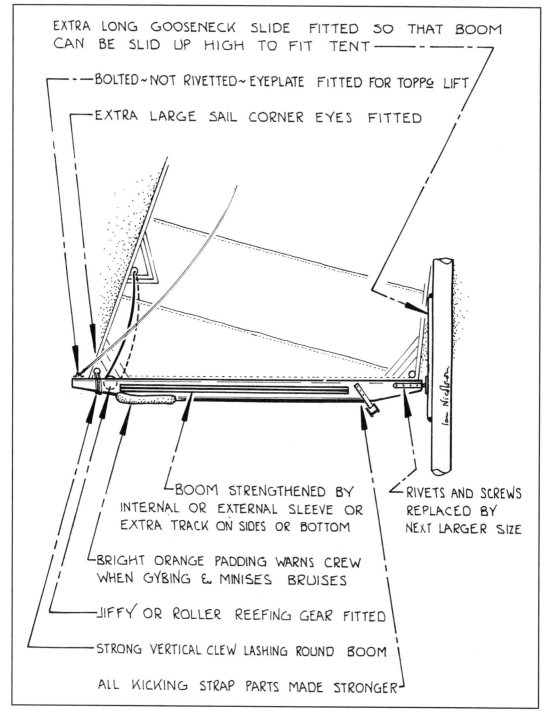

EXTRA LONG GOOSENECK SLIDE FITTED SO THAT BOOM CAN BE SLID UP HIGH TO FIT TENT

BOLTED~NOT RIVETTED~EYEPLATE FITTED FOR TOPP͌ LIFT

EXTRA LARGE SAIL CORNER EYES FITTED

BOOM STRENGTHENED BY INTERNAL OR EXTERNAL SLEEVE OR EXTRA TRACK ON SIDES OR BOTTOM

RIVETS AND SCREWS REPLACED BY NEXT LARGER SIZE

BRIGHT ORANGE PADDING WARNS CREW WHEN GYBING & MINISES BRUISES

JIFFY OR ROLLER REEFING GEAR FITTED

STRONG VERTICAL CLEW LASHING ROUND BOOM

ALL KICKING STRAP PARTS MADE STRONGER

More changes needed on a racing boat to be used for cruising

Light equipment must be altered or taken off and heavier gear fitted to stand up to the rigours of passage-making. Parts which show signs of twisting or buckling need strengthening or replacing. Fastenings are always a source of weakness and on racing dinghies are often too light for tough conditions.

A cruising dinghy needs stability and this test on a Carra 16 footer is a good one. Try this gently, otherwise a sudden ducking may result!

CHAPTER 3

Open Powerboats

Cruising in open powerboats is getting more popular, especially in sunny regions. In the eastern Mediterranean people enjoy roving about using outboard-driven inflatable dinghies. The islands and harbours are close enough together for safe dashing from one to the next when the sea is calm. The low cost of this cruising, as compared with conventional decked-boat voyaging, is just one of the attractions. The satisfaction is more solid because the achievement is bigger. But open-sea work should not be tried till the crew has ample experience in sheltered waters.

On large lakes, where the winds are fickle, powerboat cruising is more logical than sail. And on narrow winding rivers or canals, or on any waterway criss-crossed with low bridges, a powerboat makes more sense than a sailing craft. In practice, many owners of low- and moderate-speed powercraft like to have some simple sail plan, partly to deal with an engine breakdown, partly to steady the boat in rough conditions, and also to add interest to voyaging. A rig is great for youngsters who like to be active, it is good for getting radio aerials high up, it adds to the appearance of the boat, and it can be extremely useful working over shallows or through weeds when there is a risk that using the engine will trouble the propeller. Spars are also so useful for supporting a tent or cover at night.

What Type of Cruising?

Right from the start a choice has to be made between slow, medium and fast power cruising. As a rough guide, slow-speed cruising is up to about 7 or 10 knots, and medium-speed cruising up to around 25 knots. On some rivers and canals there is a speed limit which may be as low as 4 knots. This is usually to prevent the waves from boats washing away the banks.

Slow cruising is cheapest, more restful, it should be quieter and it suits small areas. Medium-speed boats can dash between harbours in short breaks between spells of bad weather. They can often get in before rough winds arrive, especially if a careful weather watch is kept by observation and radio.

Many people would not be interested in exploring a whole cruising region in the first three weekends and then having to move to another suitable stretch of coast or lake. On the other hand, some owners by nature like to cover lots of ground quickly, and do not mind putting the boat onto a trailer and moving her perhaps several hundred miles at quite frequent intervals. It is largely a matter of temperament which level of speed and activity is chosen.

High-speed open-boat cruising is specialised; it is not for beginners. Only after a couple of years' intensive experience in moderately fast boats should anyone take the next step. It is more costly, riskier, calls for a high standard of engine maintenance, needs careful planning and a rugged boat.

What Type of Boat?

Inflatable boats are popular for fast and slow cruising because they are moderately inexpensive and need little maintenance. However, the very cheap versions should be avoided as they are just toys, intended for use over a brief summer holiday. These low-price craft are made of short-life materials and they are often ruined quickly by bright sunshine or energetic usage.

There is a vast choice of open powerboats, most of which are built of fibreglass. Whether buying a second-hand boat or a new one, it is worth having the craft surveyed by a specialist. New boats come out of factories in large numbers, and far from being free from defects, it is common to find that a fault is perpetuated in every single boat which comes off the production line. Typical faults are serious blow-holes along the keel and chine lines, poor deck to hull joins, important fittings held by screws instead of bolts, inadequate reinforcing at transom edges to take outboard engine loads, and so on. Naturally, on a second-hand boat it is important to look for osmosis, or 'boat pox'. For further details about surveying, there is the standard reference book *Surveying Small Craft* by Ian Nicolson (see also *Surveying Wood Craft* by Ian Nicolson, published by the International Institute of Marine Surveying).

A good material for an open-cruising boat is aluminium. It stands up to hard use, if banged it will dent rather than hole unless the blow is massive, and it needs little maintenance. Purists like wood, and it has lots of advantages. It stands up to rough handling, it is easy to strengthen and repair, especially using epoxy resins, it is pleasant to touch and it is buoyant. If only it needed slightly less maintenance!

Anyone looking for a very cheap boat will probably find wood his best bet. He can build his own, or go for an old-timer which may well need restoring. Another way to get a cheap boat is to buy a bare hull and complete it at home. The shell can be of fibreglass, wood, aluminium or, for very hard use, steel. Guidance for working on bare hulls is given in *Build Your Own Boat* and *Improve Your Own Boat* by Ian Nicolson.

What Type of Engine?

A choice has to be made between inboard and outboard engines. The arguments are numerous and, as in so many aspects of going afloat, there are noisy enthusiasts backing both sides. Most would agree with the following lists of advantages and disadvantages:

Outboard Engines	Inboard Engines
Cost less initially.	Last longer.
Use more fuel.	Cannot be carried ashore for servicing.
Do not suffer from line-up problems.	Sound-proofing is usually easy to add.
Propeller steering is handy in small spaces and rough seas.	The weight amidships is well placed.
	Working on the engines afloat is easier.
Can be tipped to clear a fouled propeller.	Have a higher reputation for reliability.
Can be traded in for new ones, maybe larger.	Tend to be more robust.
There are plenty of accredited service stations world-wide.	Have built-in fuel systems.

The next argument to be discussed is diesel versus petrol. There are very few diesel outboards, though it is possible to get models which run on low-cost paraffin (kerosene). In some areas this fuel is hard to find.

Diesel Engines	Petrol Engines
Cost more initially.	Less reliable.
Heavy.	The weight difference is not great.
Use less fuel per mile.	In some areas petrol is easier to get, in other areas the reverse is true.
Harder to service.	Need more servicing.
Noisier.	Far bigger risk of fire or explosion.
Vibrate more.	Need more elaborate fire precautions.

In practice, the diesel market has swept Europe and is beginning to dominate the world, largely because of the reliability factor, with safety a second important influence.

Practical Considerations

During the cruise planning stage, it is vital to plot refuelling points. If a boat can go for 100 miles before she has to take on fuel, each stage must be well below this limit. Some people reckon that each jump should be no more than half the maximum range. Certainly, bad weather can make an enormous difference. A boat which is capable of 7 knots may find that with a very strong head wind and rough seas she is only just making headway. In extreme conditions, a small powerboat may be incapable of fighting to windward. I've been out in conditions many times when we had to concentrate hard to keep the bow from being blown off. When that happens it is essential to bring the helm over no more than the optimum to get the boat back on course. Typically, 17° of helm is best. Anything more and the rudder is starting to act as a brake. At over 32° the rudder certainly ceases to be a truly effective turning device and becomes more and more of a brake. For this reason there may be tiller stops at 32° to prevent the helm going over further.

With an outboard, the whole engine turns, to alter course. So in severe weather, if the bow gets blown off course, an outboard will normally drive the bow back up into the wind, but only if the engine has adequate power. So, as with any boat, the crew must always have at the back of their minds the possibility that they may have to change destinations. Alternative courses and harbours, or headlands which can be used for shelter, must be thought about well in advance.

For the ideal horsepower for a given boat you could consult the *Boat Data Book* by Ian Nicolson.

If the boat is outboard driven it is common to see a second much smaller engine carried as a spare. A better arrangement is to have two similar engines, each one of which is capable of getting the boat home against tough conditions. Two identical engines can be served by one set of spares. Whatever arrangements there are in the way of twin or stand-by engines, both outboards must be kept on the transom, ready for instant use. Most power failures occur in bad weather, and with the boat pitching about, no one is going to enjoy lugging a mass of sharp-cornered machinery about. Engines are slippery and not designed primarily for man-handling so there is always a good chance one will be dropped overboard.

A technique has to be worked out for refuelling at sea, unless all the available fuel is carried in tanks which are piped together. If portable cans are used, a very big funnel is needed. During refuelling this funnel has to be held upright, as does the fuel can. Rain and spray are collected by the funnel, and as the boat jumps about, fuel spills everywhere. It can be chaotic and wasteful, besides resulting in well-watered fuel.

A better system works something like this: the spare fuel is kept in cans which have screw-in connector pipes. These pipes fit well, so there is no leaking or splashing at either end. The main tank has a secondary filler cap which is well sheltered, possibly in a large locker or under a folding hood, even though the main filler inlet is on a side-deck or aft deck where spilt fuel can be cleaned up easily.

Spare fuel is carried in tanks which are large enough to prevent frequent refuelling, not so large that they are heavy to handle. For most people the upper size limit is 3 gallons. In a 12 ft boat being tossed about a 1 gallon can is quite a handful.

In a power-driven open boat, the wind is almost always from ahead so some form of weather protection is needed. A windscreen should extend right to the side of the boat to prevent rain and spray driving round the ends and wetting the helmsman. If it is high enough most moisture will fly over his head, except when the wind is from astern and almost as fast or faster than the boat's speed. A fully enclosed steering position is what we all need when the weather is foul, but it limits the enjoyment in perfect weather. No wonder so many boats have folding hoods over the helmsman's seat.

In outboard-driven boats the helmsman should not sit right aft. If he has a tiller extension, or a steering wheel set roughly one third of the length from the transom, he will be away from the worst of the noise. Just as important, his weight will be better placed raising the freeboard at the transom and so making the boat safer. She may even be faster too. In addition, he will probably have a better view forward and the motion may be slightly less. He will also be within reach of more equipment.

The Drascombe Lugger has a special transom forward of the stem for the outboard. This protects the engine in crowded harbours and makes it easier to ship the engine, work on it and lift it when not in use.

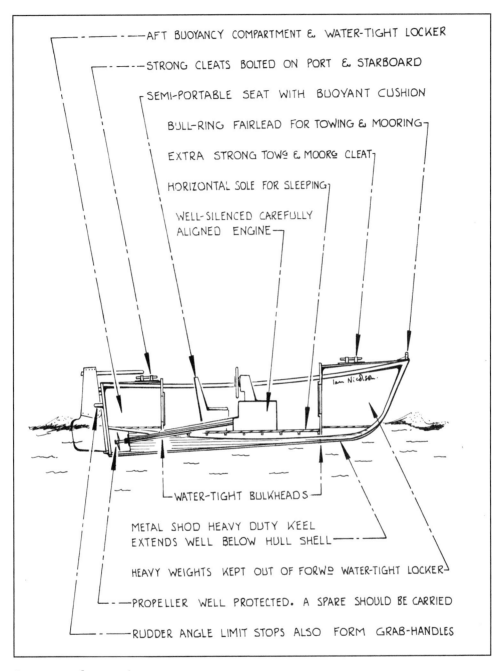

AFT BUOYANCY COMPARTMENT & WATER-TIGHT LOCKER

STRONG CLEATS BOLTED ON PORT & STARBOARD

SEMI-PORTABLE SEAT WITH BUOYANT CUSHION

BULL-RING FAIRLEAD FOR TOWING & MOORING

EXTRA STRONG TOWG & MOORG CLEAT

HORIZONTAL SOLE FOR SLEEPING

WELL-SILENCED CAREFULLY ALIGNED ENGINE

WATER-TIGHT BULKHEADS

METAL SHOD HEAVY DUTY KEEL EXTENDS WELL BELOW HULL SHELL

HEAVY WEIGHTS KEPT OUT OF FORWD WATER-TIGHT LOCKER

PROPELLER WELL PROTECTED. A SPARE SHOULD BE CARRIED

RUDDER ANGLE LIMIT STOPS ALSO FORM GRAB-HANDLES

Open powerboat cruiser

Safety, comfort and reliability are the qualities needed for this boat. Unless the voyaging is in very sheltered waters, a boat which will float even when flooded is best. Some of the modern self-bailing boats are ideal, provided water does not get between the inner and outer hull shells.

A quietened engine and comfortable seating are desirable and not hard to achieve. All the deck fittings should be outsize, and bolted down to strong under-deck pads. Everything possible should be duplicated, including bilge pump, anchor, and some people even carry a reserve outboard engine in case the main engine fails.

Boats used for cruising need more safety gear and more protective scantlings than those which are just taken out for the occasional zip round the harbour. For instance, there should be a metal band along the keel to minimise trouble when grounding. Some form of deck-edge protection is advisable to help the fenders when lying alongside, and one fender for every 3 ft (1 m) of boat length. Even the smallest boat needs a minimum of five fenders as well as a very good cleat, or better still two, at the bow ... and likewise aft, as well as strong points for securing the fenders.

The underside of an inflatable boat may be protected by two parallel keels of hardwood on edge and bolted through, with matching wood stiffeners forming long 'plate washers' on the inside. The outside rubbing pieces will on a 12 ft (3.7 m) boat probably run for two-thirds the length of the boat and be 1½ in × 2 in, (40 mm × 50 mm) in section with well-rounded-up fore ends. Bronze bolts, ⅜ in (8 mm) diameter at 10 in (250 mm) centres should be ample. For very rough beaches the rubbing pieces may be 4 in (100 mm) deep or more and shod with bronze strips. These will typically be ⅛ in (3 mm) thick and slightly narrower than the wood, held at 6 in (150 mm) intervals by well countersunk 1 in (25 mm) 10 gauge screws.

The ideal open powerboat has enough buoyancy in the form of tanks, inflated bags, or sealed compartments to ensure she easily floats when flooded. When filled with water there should be ample freeboard, despite the load of crew and gear, so that she can be bailed out faster than water blows back aboard.

In windy weather a self-bailer or two are helpful though they require constant policing, otherwise dirt will seep under the lips and water will get in when the boat stops. A man-sized bilge pump, not a toy, is what is wanted. It is best located so that the helmsman can work it. All the safety gear, as well as the boat cover, cooking equipment, clothes and so on are much the same as for a sailing boat. Extra items include ear plugs if the engine is noisy, sea-going engine spares, a comprehensive set of engine tools, engine manuals, a list of engine agents in the cruising ground, a spare propeller, unless perhaps the spare engine covers this, and spare lubricating oil.

CHAPTER 4

Rigs

The Bermudan Rig

The ordinary Bermudan rig with mainsail and jib is so common, so well developed and so easy to use and to adjust to different conditions, that it dominates the sailing world.

A typical cruising dinghy will have a mainsail about twice the size of the jib, and the best boats will sail well (though a lot slower) when the jib is lowered. This means that when coming into a strange harbour, or in a sudden squall or in an emergency, the headsail is dropped and the boat becomes more docile. The view forward is also improved and as there are then no jib sheets to handle, tacking involves just pulling the helm over. If there are two in the boat, the jib sheet hand can concentrate on navigating, or shouting to the harbour master for information about where to moor.

On most boats the Bermudan rig will have a single shroud each side and a single forestay. It is a good idea to do without rigging screws because they are vulnerable and not cheap. Better alternatives for cruising are lashings or stay adjuster plates. The former should be multiple turns of ⅛ in (3 mm) diameter Terylene (Dacron), using enough turns to ensure that the lashing is as strong as the wire. Here, as elsewhere, when the strength of any boat's rigging or other technical information is needed, a useful source is *The Boat Data Book* by Ian Nicolson.

Lashings need regular inspection for chafe and cautious sailors use two lashings on each shroud, so that if one chafes through, the other will hold. They stretch and need re-tying every time the mast is set up, so the length of the lashing may vary on each occasion, which is a slight nuisance.

Stay adjuster plates get over the disadvantage of lashings. They are pairs of stainless steel plates with a row of holes. A clevis pin goes through the first plate, then through the eye at the bottom of the shroud, then through the second plate. There is no risk that chafe will eat through these plates. Once it has been established by trial which hole in the length of the plates suits the boat best, it is easy to set the rig up in exactly the same way month after month.

The mast of a Bermudan rig extends far beyond the bow and stem when laid on the hull or trailer for travelling. This is a constant worry, so various arrangements have been devised to make it possible to divide the mast into two. Some work well, some are horrible, all depend on careful handling and good engineering. All should be treated with caution and inspected frequently. The most common consists of a sleeve fixed permanently inside the lower section of the spar. The upper part of the mast slides over and, as the mast is oval, no device is needed to line up the parts. If the sleeve or the base of the upper part of the mast gets dented or scarred, the two pieces of mast may refuse to slide together. If corrosion occurs, it may take hours of bashing and swearing to get the two sections together, or to separate them. A careful application of Vaseline or lanolin will help to keep corrosion away and help the two parts to slide together or apart. A wrapping of cloth or plastic buckets fixed over each end when they are separated will reduce the chances of damage.

A principal source of trouble is the luff groove because it gets bashed sideways and closed. The mating ends should be slightly belled out to help the luff of the mainsail slide up past the join. Internal halliards are to be avoided with a divided mast. For that matter, a remarkably good case can be made for not having divided masts. They cause almost as much trouble, and sometimes more, than they are intended to save.

Single-handers and people who suffer from the aches and pains normally associated with advancing age should seriously consider having a self-tacking jib. This headsail does not extend aft of the mast, so its area will be smaller than usual, but its sheet is attached to a track or length of wire athwartships across the aft end of the foredeck. When the helm is put over to tack, the headsail changes sides just like the mainsail, without any intervention on the part of the crew.

Self-tacking headsails would be more popular if it were possible to have some area in the sail extending back behind the mast. Since this is not possible, these sails tend to be high and narrow, so they often need battens. Some have full width battens which are good for efficiency but they need extra care and maintenance.

The 15-foot (4.5-metre) Drascombe Scaffie has a real cruising rig, with a boomless lugsail which has three sensible reefs. She is built by Honnor Marine.

Another disadvantage is that there is no weather sheet to haul tight for heaving to, or slowing the boat down, or backing the headsail to make the boat pay off on a particular tack. It is easy to fit light lines to the traveller on the track (or to the sail's clew) leading out and round the shrouds, one line each side, so that the sail can be pulled across. Admittedly such extra ropes are a nuisance and nothing like as quickly and easily worked as ordinary sheets.

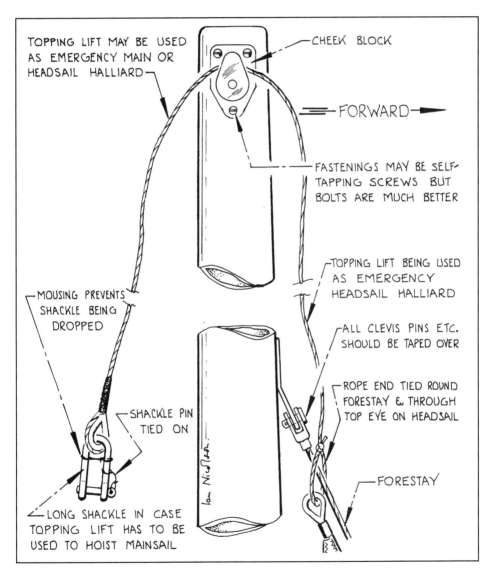

TOPPING LIFT MAY BE USED AS EMERGENCY MAIN OR HEADSAIL HALLIARD

CHEEK BLOCK

FORWARD

FASTENINGS MAY BE SELF-TAPPING SCREWS BUT BOLTS ARE MUCH BETTER

TOPPING LIFT BEING USED AS EMERGENCY HEADSAIL HALLIARD

MOUSING PREVENTS SHACKLE BEING DROPPED

ALL CLEVIS PINS ETC. SHOULD BE TAPED OVER

ROPE END TIED ROUND FORESTAY & THROUGH TOP EYE ON HEADSAIL

SHACKLE PIN TIED ON

FORESTAY

LONG SHACKLE IN CASE TOPPING LIFT HAS TO BE USED TO HOIST MAINSAIL

Topping lift doubles as emergency halliard

Provided the masthead block is correctly sited, the topping lift can be used to hoist the mainsail or a headsail, when a normal halliard fails. This arrangement can be added to most masts, and the topping lift will also be used, very often, to support the boom which, in turn, holds the tent up over the boat.

The Una Rig

The Una rig consists of a Bermudan mainsail with no headsail. A single-hander may find it suits him, in spite of its lack of flexibility and the relative awkwardness of reefing. It is quite common for this rig to have no shrouds and this is certainly an asset in that there are fewer parts to maintain, fewer things to go wrong and less windage aloft. Best of all, in a squall when running, the whole sail can be let off forward of the mast to reduce the forces on the boat. Naturally, this can only be done if the gooseneck allows the boom to go round the mast. However, if the squall refuses to die away, the boat may be in real trouble. It will be hard to lower the sail and if the boat rounds up into the wind unreefed, she is likely to capsize. On balance, the Una rig is seldom entirely satisfactory for cruising.

Basic Guide to Rigs

There are so many other possible rigs and variations of rigs that whole books have been written on the subject. Amid the welter of information certain basic principles stand out:

1. High, narrow rigs are good for going to windward.
2. Low rigs are less efficient but less likely to cause a capsize.
3. The further away from the Bermudan rig, the less easy is it to get parts and spares. Any chandler stocks a selection of slides, goosenecks, kicking straps and so on. Many keep a few stock spars. If the rig is 'non-standard', the spars may have to be specially made, probably out of wood.
4. Once the boat sails 'off the beaten track' where there are no chandlers, unusual rigs come more into their own. They are often easy to repair with simple tools.
5. The more sails there are, the more adaptable the rig; but it will cost more to buy and run.

The Gunter Rig

The gunter rig is half cousin to the ordinary Bermudan sloop. Instead of a tall mast there is a gaff and shortish mast. The gaff is almost vertical and is pulled tight up to the mast; it may have one halliard or two. It is rare that the rig is adjusted right first time and to be set properly it tends to need occasional changes as the mainsail stretches, or the band holding the gaff close to the mast wears. However, it is a good rig if the boat has to stay afloat all the time, and all the spars usually stow within the length of the hull. This helps when trailing behind a car. An existing Bermudan mainsail can sometimes be rather crudely altered to fit a gunter rig and the spars are easily made or repaired by a competent amateur.

The Lug Rig

A lug sail is four-sided, the top of the sail being laced to a spar which is hoisted up the mast. This spar is the gaff and it may overlap the mast slightly and stay on the same side of the mast all the time, in which case it is called a 'standing' lug. Alternatively the gaff can extend forward of the mast about ⅔ths of its length, in which case it is called a 'dipping lug' because the fore end of the gaff is dipped round behind the mast each time the boat tacks. This is not a perfectly simple manoeuvre, certainly not for a single-hander working in a rough sea with rather too much wind about.

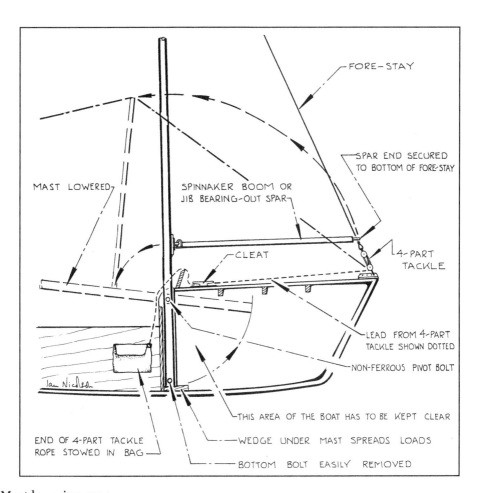

FORE-STAY

SPAR END SECURED TO BOTTOM OF FORE-STAY

MAST LOWERED

SPINNAKER BOOM OR JIB BEARING-OUT SPAR

4-PART TACKLE

CLEAT

LEAD FROM 4-PART TACKLE SHOWN DOTTED

NON-FERROUS PIVOT BOLT

Ian Nicolson

THIS AREA OF THE BOAT HAS TO BE KEPT CLEAR

END OF 4-PART TACKLE ROPE STOWED IN BAG

WEDGE UNDER MAST SPREADS LOADS

BOTTOM BOLT EASILY REMOVED

Mast-lowering gear
The mast must stand in a 'tabernacle' if it is to be easy to lower in all weathers. A simple mast-heel pivot can be used but it is less reliable than a tall box-shaped 'tabernacle' with strong sides and back, as shown here. A spar, such as the spinnaker pole, is used as a strut, otherwise when the mast is nearly down the angle between it and the forestay is too small and the load on the lowering tackle too high.

The bolts holding the mast may be tubular to save weight, and can be simple pieces of tube with washers and split pins at each end.

Having owned two standing lugsail cruising dinghies, I'm biased in their favour because they are cheap to run, easy to rig, great on a reach or run, the spars stow inside the boat and they can be used with no boom or partial boom. They are poor to windward compared with the Bermudan rig, but then it's often more sense, more fun and cheaper to cruise downwind.

Other Rigs

Sprit-sail rigged boats are rare, but the sail and spars are not hard for an amateur to make and usually all spars stow inside the boat, provided the sprit does not extend right down to near the gooseneck. Anyone who cruises on rivers or canals where it is often necessary to duck under low bridges should go for this rig, or one of the non-Bermudan ones.

Two-masted open boats are relatively rare, but becoming more popular. Some have spars short enough to stow inboard, some have only main and mizzen which are both self-tacking – so handy if one of the crew is cooking or navigating – some are just Bermudan rigs with a mizzen added to give extra flexibility with smaller, more easily handled mainsails.

Yawls can be a nuisance because the mizzen and all its parts are so far aft they are partially out beyond the stern. In confined harbours this can be irritating if not downright damaging. If anything goes wrong at sea it can be hard or impossible to reach far enough aft to cure the crisis. The extending boom usually needs a bumpkin to take the lower mizzen sheet block and this outreaching spar may interfere with the outboard engine. In rough conditions it is pleasant to be able to sail under headsail and mizzen, but this still means that the headsail sheets have to be handled at each tack. As a result some crews prefer to sail under main only, lowering the forward and aft ones to reduce the total area. This argument about whether the best bad-weather rig is 'mainsail only' or 'jib-and-mizzen' only applies to both ketches and yawls. It is a disagreement which has raged for centuries and, like others in the sailing world, it depends largely on the performance and attributes of the boat under discussion. Each owner has to make his own cautious experiments. Having owned two ketches, I have found that there are times when it pays to reef all three sails to get the best out of the boat, so there are in practice three options. This means that all three, main, mizzen and headsail should all be reefable, which adds more to the cost. Of course, two-masters must always be more expensive than single-stick boats.

CHAPTER 5

Sails

The sails are the engine of a wind-driven boat. They need as much care as the machinery which drives any vehicle ... yet, in practice, they often suffer terrible neglect. They start off life at a disadvantage (so far as a cruising dinghy is concerned) because they are usually wrongly made. Most dinghy sails are made for racing, in which case the sole consideration is speed. Longevity, reserve strength, quick reefing, resistance to accidents, and the ability to withstand weather are forgotten. After all, racing dinghies do not go out in screeching winds, but a cruising boat may be caught out in such conditions and the last thing needed then is a rent across a sail.

Those sails not made for racing are mass-produced horrors for standard dinghies. Here the sole criterion is cheapness. The market in dinghies is so competitive that every component must be made as cheaply as possible. No thought is given to longevity, reserve strength ... here we go again!

In our sail loft we were saddened every year when we saw the inadequate sails which are sold with new dinghies. Stout cruising dinghies, such as are used at Outward Bound camps and sailing schools, are marketed with sails which after a couple of full seasons' use are virtually scrap. These sails are too light, poorly finished, made with under-strength components and not designed to stand up to the hurly-burly of life afloat ... certainly not life outside the shelter of harbour.

Sails for Cruising

It's true that specially made cruising sails will have a higher first cost than standard mass-produced ones, but taking a three or four year view, the specials will be cheaper and give better cruising.

Cloth weight should be high. Typically, a 16 ft (5 m) boat should have cloth around 5 oz weight, and for really extended cruising it should be about 5.7 oz. Certainly an 18 ft (5.5 m) boat should have 5.7 oz sails. In each case the headsail may be a little less.

The corner patches should be larger than usual and, for really tough going, I like the bottom reinforcing to extend about 20 per cent along the foot from the luff and the leech. Such blatant extra strength gives peace of mind when the wind howls and shrieks in the rigging.

For very extended cruising the sailmaker might be asked for triple stitching, though this is seldom seen on small boat sails. For decked yachts which make long voyages it is a normal precaution.

There are some excellent plastic headboards, but they are still only plastic. Aluminium headboards are stronger and, if a sailmaker does not stock them, they are easy to make. If a plastic headboard simply has to be used, the hole for the main halliard should be bushed with metal to prevent wear and ovalising of the hole. An owner can do this job using a piece of copper tube.

The luff of the mainsail and mizzen must have slides which fit in a mast track or groove; otherwise when the sail is lowered it drops in a bundle into the boat or blows overboard. Slides keep the sail onto the mast and make it easy to stow on the boom. The foot of these sails can be fitted with a boltrope which goes in a groove along

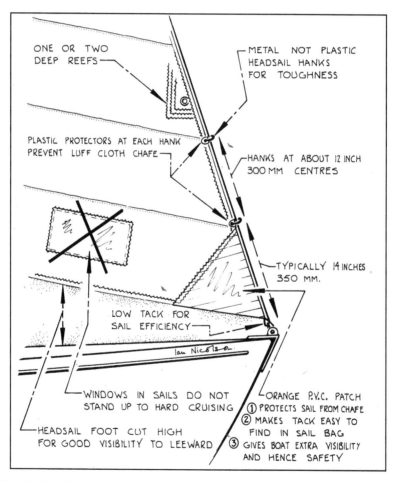

ONE OR TWO DEEP REEFS

METAL NOT PLASTIC HEADSAIL HANKS FOR TOUGHNESS

PLASTIC PROTECTORS AT EACH HANK PREVENT LUFF CLOTH CHAFE

HANKS AT ABOUT 12 INCH 300 MM CENTRES

TYPICALLY 14 INCHES 350 MM.

LOW TACK FOR SAIL EFFICIENCY

Ian Nicolson.

WINDOWS IN SAILS DO NOT STAND UP TO HARD CRUISING

HEADSAIL FOOT CUT HIGH FOR GOOD VISIBILITY TO LEEWARD

ORANGE P.V.C. PATCH
① PROTECTS SAIL FROM CHAFE
② MAKES TACK EASY TO FIND IN SAIL BAG
③ GIVES BOAT EXTRA VISIBILITY AND HENCE SAFETY

Headsail tack details

Cruising sails are very different from racing sails, and should be at least one weight heavier, to give long reliable service. Speed has to be sacrificed to safety, comfort and convenience sometimes, but the sails should still be designed to give the boat a good performance. No one likes to go slowly.

the boom, but there must be some arrangement to prevent the loading at the leech from pulling the aft end of the foot out of the boom track. The best technique is to tie the clew eye round the boom as well as hauling it aft, though this makes it hard or impossible to vary the tension of the foot when under way. Three turns of ⅛ in (3 mm) line makes a good lashing.

Those metal 'slugs', sometimes called 'clew sliders', which fit on the aft end of the sail foot and are specially designed to prevent the clew from tearing out of the track, have been known to burst out of the track. They can, in extreme conditions, force the track sides apart by their wedging action.

There must be two slides on the headboard, and all slides need attaching with shackles or tape sewn through, or one of the other long-lasting techniques which are so much better than the old-fashioned method of sewing them on.

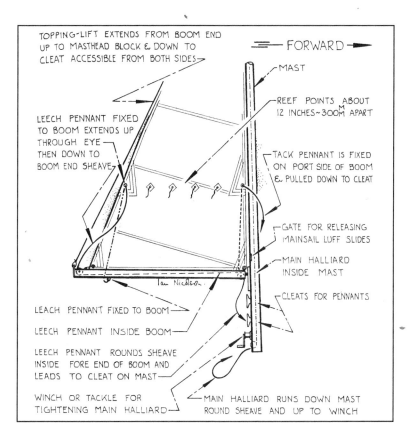

Jiffy reefing

There are different ways of arranging quick, safe reefing, and this sketch shows some important details. The main reefing lines and the main halliard can be led aft along the top of the centreboard case, so that one of the crew can carry out a quick reef from amidships. In this sketch the ropes are led to cleats on the aft side of the mast so that they are easily reached from port or starboard. Both the reefing pennants can have tackles to give extra power, the one on the leech downhaul being inside the boom. The luff pennant seldom needs a tackle as the sail just drops down the mast, and the luff is tightened with the winch or main halliard tackle.

In the same way, headsail hanks must be the metal kind, not those light plastic substitutes which are fine for racing because they weigh little, but they do not stand up to rough cruising conditions.

I prefer the stainless steel hanks and have found they have little tendency to corrode, whereas the bronze ones seize too often. If bronze ones are used, they must be greased with lanoline every two months.

The disadvantage of stainless steel hanks is that they usually have to be sewn on, whereas at least one type of bronze hank has a metal tail which passes through the sail eyelet and is then hammered closed. Whatever type of hank is used, there should be plastic protectors between it and the sail luff and that's something seldom found on cheap mass mismade sails.

Corner eyes must be the kind that are hydraulically pressed in, never the soft hammered type. On a 16 ft (5 m) boat they should be ½ in (12 mm) inside diameter, and the next size up, ⅝ in (15 mm) is not too large for serious cruising. The same applies to reefing eyes where the larger size makes the reefing lines run just that little bit more easily.

Battens

Batten pockets fail earlier than other parts of sail, so a cooperative sailmaker might be asked to make them extra wide, then an extra row of stitching can be worked all round. In rough conditions battens flip out of the kind of pocket which has a piece of elastic at the fore end.

This stretching tape also has a short life when exposed to sunshine, so it elongates and becomes useless before other parts of the sail are worn. For this reason it is best to have old-fashioned battens which are tied in. Ideally the batten pocket openings are sewn over.

Modern battens all sink when they fall overboard and a good case can be made for having homemade wooden ones. Traditionally these were made of hickory, but as this is not always available, ash is used instead. The batten width should be about ¹⁄₁₄₀th of the boat's length and the thickness about ³⁄₁₆ in (4 mm) for a 16 ft (5 m) dinghy tapering down to less than ⅛ in at the fore end.

All edges and corners need to be very well rounded to prevent chafe in the pocket. Three battens are usual and, as a basic rule, they will give good service if they are about ¼ as long as the boom, with the top one full length.

One advantage of ample battens, which are also of good length, is that they will support extra sail area in the leech. For cruising this is an asset because it gives good down-wind and reaching performance; most crews will aim to be on those points of sailing as much as possible. Just as important, a low rig is advantageous for cruising, but without a well-rounded leech it may be short in total sail area.

Reefs

As jiffy reefs are fairly expensive, a good case can be made for having only two of them. Besides, most people reef too late, so a large reduction is required by the time the crew get round to reducing sail, especially if the wind is gusting up the Beaufort Scale, missing out the odd numbers.

In practice, a small first reef is seldom used by cruising people, who rightly feel that a modest reduction in area does not suit those black clouds tumbling up across the heavens. So what makes sense, though at first sight it does look sombre and pessimistic, is a reef ⅕ up the luff and a second one ⅖ up. In each case it is a good idea to angle the reef up at the aft end, so that the boom is raised above the horizontal by about 5 degrees for each reef. This gives extra visibility to leeward and extra headroom under the boom too.

If the boat is fitted with roller reefing, there shout be one emergency reef about ⅖ up the luff in case the reefing gear fails.

Sail Colour and Type

Sails are normally white, but the glare off the brilliant shiny cloth is hard on the eyes in bright sunshine. This is one reason why some owners prefer the tan colour, even though it is more costly. It tends to fade in time, especially if continually exposed to sunlight.

When at sea, dinghies are surprisingly hard to see; as a result it is possible to capsize a few miles from a coastguard station or busy and well populated town, yet be unnoticed. Coloured sails therefore make sense. The best colours are bright orange, red, a mustard yellow and, in some conditions, blue seems to show up well.

It has to be admitted that coloured cloth is not widely available and some small sailmakers do not like to stock it because they cannot use it often, so it lies on their shelves year after year. What seems to matter is that there should be more than one colour in the sails. So one might go for a tan top panel, as a basic minimum, and have all the other cloths white. Some sails are made with alternate white and coloured cloths and these do show up well, even in the fading light of dusk.

If a boat carries a heavy-weather headsail, a good case can be made for having it in that violently bright yellow/orange cloth, which is specially sold for storm headsails, provided it can be bought in a suitable cloth weight. Few cruising dinghies will carry jibs for severe conditions unless they are 18 ft (5.5 m) long or more. For limited cruising a better arrangement is to have a reef in the jib, because this can be put in quickly and it reduces the amount of gear carried in the overcrowded available space.

Tough owners who like to cover a lot of miles may be tempted to have light-weather sails. A spinnaker does not take up much space, being made of nylon which compresses down and stows in a small bag. But it does need a complete set of gear, including sheets, a boom with up-haul and down-haul and mast fitting, extra cleats and a special halliard. Admittedly, the halliard can double as an emergency headsail halliard or even a main boom topping lift. However, a topping lift which goes to the top of the forestay is less easy to use than one which goes to the masthead. If a spinnaker is carried, it is best to have a flat one. It will be easier to set and carry in difficult wind conditions, it will go on working as the wind comes round on the beam, and it is likely to be a bit cheaper too. There used to be a fashion for nylon reaching genoas because they were light and easily stowed, cost less than Terylene (Dacron)

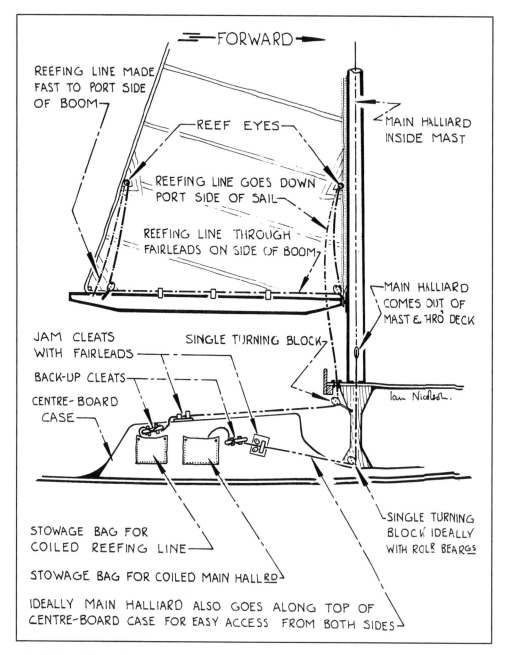

REEFING LINE MADE FAST TO PORT SIDE OF BOOM

REEF EYES

REEFING LINE GOES DOWN PORT SIDE OF SAIL

REEFING LINE THROUGH FAIRLEADS ON SIDE OF BOOM

MAIN HALLIARD INSIDE MAST

MAIN HALLIARD COMES OUT OF MAST & THRO DECK

JAM CLEATS WITH FAIRLEADS

BACK-UP CLEATS

CENTRE-BOARD CASE

SINGLE TURNING BLOCK

Ian Nicolson.

STOWAGE BAG FOR COILED REEFING LINE

SINGLE TURNING BLOCK IDEALLY WITH ROLR BEARGS

STOWAGE BAG FOR COILED MAIN HALL RD

IDEALLY MAIN HALLIARD ALSO GOES ALONG TOP OF CENTRE-BOARD CASE FOR EASY ACCESS FROM BOTH SIDES

FORWARD

Single-line jiffy reefing

By letting off the main halliard and hauling on a single reefing line, this system gives quick, simple reefing.

The reefing line starts where it is made fast at the aft end of the boom, on the port side; it runs up the port side of the sail, through the eye, and down the starboard side to a block aft of the eye, then either along the inside of the boom, or through fairleads on the outside, as shown here. Next, it goes through a block, up the starboard side, and through the luff eye, down the port side of the sail, to a turning block which takes it to a jam cleat and stowage at the aft end of the centreboard case.

Both the main halliard and the reefing line have back-up cleats in case the jam cleats fail.

sails, and were effective once the wind was clearly on the beam. What probably killed them was the way owners insisted on using them when the wind was too far ahead, and the price difference is not all that significant. But for anyone trying to get a slow dinghy to liven up, one could be worth considering, especially if it were combined with a bearing out spar, so that downwind the sail would be set on the opposite side to the main. The spar would probably double as a sounding pole, described in chapter 14 on special equipment.

Devices which improve the performance of a sail also put up the cost. Each owner will make up his own mind if he wants Cunningham holes, in main or headsail. On balance they are not recommended unless the crew are keen to get extra mileage every day. However, tell-tales on the sails can be so easily added by the owner after the sailmaker has delivered the sails, and they do make sense.

Windows in sails are a mixed blessing. If the headsail and boom are both low, they are necessary, but they wear out more quickly than the rest of the sail and need extra care when the sails are being stowed or folded. On balance, it is best to do without them if possible.

A sail number is worth having because it is easy to see from a great distance and it identifies the boat. If the boat is not one of an established class, and so does not have a number allocated by a class organisation, she might have the owner's initials on the mainsail. The standard size of numbers for a dinghy will be the ones the sailmaker will automatically use, but if the aim is to be seen and recognised from a long way off, it is logical to go for the next size up. These days the numbers are stuck on, each digit being supplied by the wholesaler with its own sticky backing. In a year or two of hard sailing the edges of the numbers tend to start peeling, so a sailmaker should be asked to sew all round the perimeter of each figure.

All sails used for cruising need to be, above everything, convenient to use. For instance, the lower batten should be set well above the first reef and should be horizontal so that it snugs down with the next reef. And even if roller reefing is fitted, the batten should still be horizontal because that makes it easier to remove. If by accident it is left in (when reefing in the dark and under stress the crew forget the batten) then the sail will roll down, even if there is some sail torturing due to the batten still being in the pocket.

Likewise, each corner and reef eye should be named with a broad, indelible pen. Plenty of experienced people have set jibs upside down when working at dawn after a sleepless night, or have tied down the No. 1 reef at the luff but the No. 2 at the leech. Here, as elsewhere, the gear has to be made proof against extremes of tiredness, darkness and bad weather.

It is common to have one bag for both main and jib. The bag may be made partly of the same cloth as the sails and then it can be used for patching. It must be so large that both sails can be put in easily without trouble, even when the sails are not folded and are sopping wet. This means that for a typical 16 footer (5 m) the bag should be 2 ft (600 mm) in width and 3 ft (1 m) in height. It is sometimes the practice to have a waterproof bag which, of course, means it is not suitable for cutting up for patching a sail, but it can then be used for stowing gear like sleeping bags when under way.

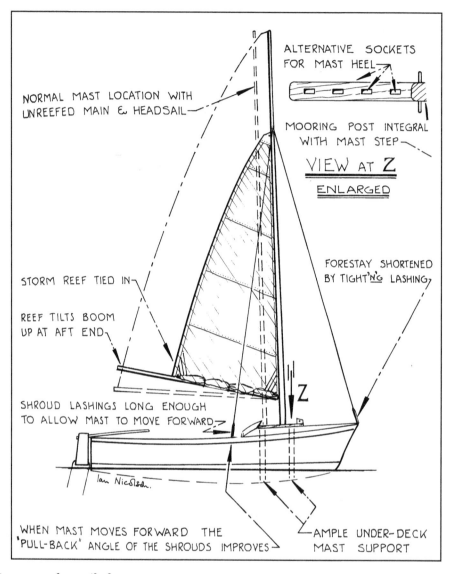

NORMAL MAST LOCATION WITH UNREEFED MAIN & HEADSAIL

ALTERNATIVE SOCKETS FOR MAST HEEL

MOORING POST INTEGRAL WITH MAST STEP

VIEW AT Z
ENLARGED

STORM REEF TIED IN

REEF TILTS BOOM UP AT AFT END

FORESTAY SHORTENED BY TIGHT'NG LASHING

SHROUD LASHINGS LONG ENOUGH TO ALLOW MAST TO MOVE FORWARD

Z

Ian Nicolson.

WHEN MAST MOVES FORWARD THE 'PULL-BACK' ANGLE OF THE SHROUDS IMPROVES

AMPLE UNDER-DECK MAST SUPPORT

Heavy-weather sail plan

When cruising, enough sail area is set to cope with the gusts, even if the boat is slightly under-canvassed in the lulls. By leaving the jib off, and moving the mast forward, sail balance is maintained when a deep reef is tied down. The forestay must have a long lashing when the mast is in its normal position, so that it can be shortened as the mast is moved forward, without the bottom eye of the forestay coming right down to the stemhead.

The sails will seldom be put in the bag when cruising, but they should always be kept in it at other times to keep the sunlight off them.

There is controversy about taking sail-repair tape on a cruise. In theory it's a great way to mend a sail, since it is quick and easy to use. However, it is seldom satisfactory when the sail is saturated and it makes the sailmaker's job more difficult when he is later doing a proper repair. It is better to learn how to make good sail repairs with palm and needle (which work almost regardless of how wet the sail is) and do without the tape.

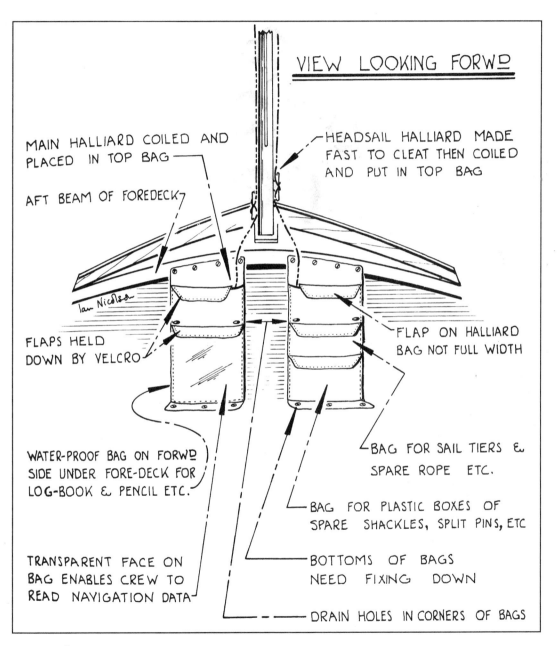

Handy stowage
Pockets or pouches made from 10 oz Terylene, perhaps coloured so that it does not show the dirt, or made of PVC cloth, can be made up by a local sailmaker. The sets shown here do not prevent the crew reaching the area under the foredeck where bulky things are stowed.

CHAPTER 6

Oars, Paddles and Outboards

When the wind dies the boat stops, unless the tide helps her along. If the tide is foul and the water too deep for anchoring, the boat goes backwards. With no serious schedule, this can be acceptable, but if the end of the holiday is nearing, or if there is a danger astern into which the tide is taking the boat, then oars have to be used.

Even when there is wind, there are locations where oars are essential. Some launching places are encompassed by breakwaters or other obstructions, so that even the smallest, handiest boat cannot beat out between them. Some rivers are so narrow that there is not space for a boat to tack back and forth, though it is amazing what can be done if the crew are patient and bear away as much as possible, however briefly, to get speed for each tack. Going against the wind down a very narrow channel it is usually fatal to pinch.

In practice, rowing can be enjoyable or hellish, according to the layout of the boat, the proportions of the oars and the amount of practice put into the job. Most sailing dinghies are not designed for rowing and those that are seldom have gear which is better than 'just adequate'. So when taking over a boat, it is common for the rowing arrangements to need making or renewing.

The seat must be rigid, which almost certainly means there must be a vertical central support at least 6 in (150 mm) fore and aft and ½ in (12 mm) thick, glued and screwed top and bottom. This scantling does not vary with the size of boat, since it is the weight and energy of the rower which has to be absorbed. A thin thwart will need stiffening and this should be done on the forward and aft edges with battens glued and screwed on the underside. If in doubt, use 1 in x 1 in (25 mm x 25 mm) hardwood, glued all along and screwed at 6 in (150 mm) centres. A seat cushion helps reduce blisters and makes rowing more enjoyable, and this can be a life ring if it is made of closed-cell foam plastic with grab lines all round. The rowlocks must be kept high, so that the oars do not touch the gunwale or the inside of the side decks, and the chocks which raise the rowlocks can also act as local stiffeners. They must be well rounded and tapered away at the ends, otherwise the crew sitting on the side decks will have an uncomfortable time.

The powerful tug of the oarsman has to be taken by strong structure and the gunwale is the nearest unit capable of standing up to the surprisingly severe forces. So even if the rowlocks are well inboard, the stiffening should tie into the gunwale.

Rowlocks must have either deep pipe sockets or upper and lower rings to hold the shank and prevent any movement except rotation. Sloppy rowlocks are as miserable as empty whisky bottles. Somewhere there may be good reliable, plastic rowlocks but so many different kinds have sheered just when the going has got tough that experienced oarsmen keep going back to metal ones. Safety lines on rowlocks should be through drilled holes at the top of the crutch because lines spliced round the necks come adrift occasionally. More rowlocks are lost overboard than wear out.

The sketch shows details of how the various components of the rowing gear should be made and spaced. Before finalising anything it is best to put everything in place but only temporarily secured, and have a trial afloat. Try other boats too, to see how they are laid out. There may be times when the oarsman has to keep up his stroke for hours on end, and comfort is all. It can be highly satisfying to make a boat go a long way in a reasonable time – or it can be a blistering hell.

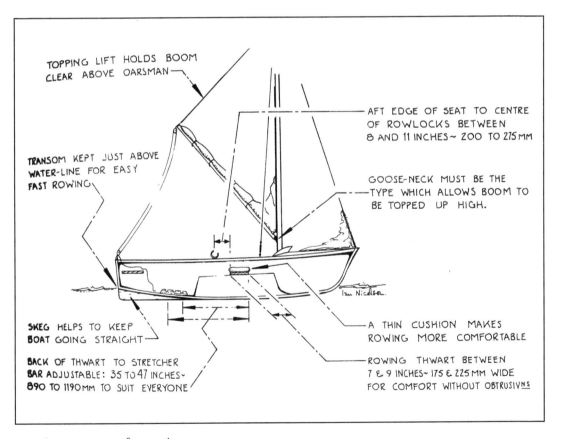

TOPPING LIFT HOLDS BOOM CLEAR ABOVE OARSMAN

AFT EDGE OF SEAT TO CENTRE OF ROWLOCKS BETWEEN 8 AND 11 INCHES~ 200 TO 275MM

TRANSOM KEPT JUST ABOVE WATER-LINE FOR EASY FAST ROWING

GOOSE-NECK MUST BE THE TYPE WHICH ALLOWS BOOM TO BE TOPPED UP HIGH.

SKEG HELPS TO KEEP BOAT GOING STRAIGHT

A THIN CUSHION MAKES ROWING MORE COMFORTABLE

BACK OF THWART TO STRETCHER BAR ADJUSTABLE: 35 TO 47 INCHES~ 890 TO 1190MM TO SUIT EVERYONE

ROWING THWART BETWEEN 7 & 9 INCHES~ 175 & 225MM WIDE FOR COMFORT WITHOUT OBTRUSIVNS

Arrangements for rowing

Rowing can be hard work, so the facilities must be right. Boats without rowlock sockets often need strengthening at the gunwhales and wider thwarts.

The cushion can double as a lifebuoy and pillow. When rowing, the boom must be well clear of the oarsman, and it is usually best to top it up rather than remove it from the gooseneck.

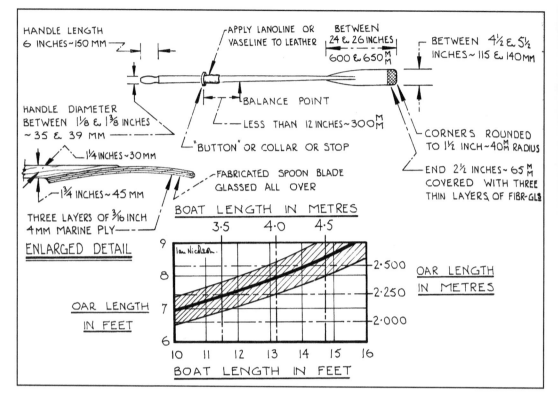

Types of oar

Long oars should result in fast progress, but small oars are easier to stow, easier to buy and less likely to get broken. Almost regardless of size, the blade area does not vary much, and the blade end needs ample protection.

Spoon-bladed oars are expensive so the enlarged detail shows how to make them easily. Just bend thin ply round a former and glue it together with epoxy resin, then round all edges and cover with fibreglass.

Rowing Technique

The oars should not be tightly grasped, even when feathering. The rower keeps his back straight, pushes with his legs and leans back on the oars. I like to use the longest stroke which is comfortable, but vary the length of stroke slightly after some time has elapsed, to reduce fatigue. In a short, steep sea it may be necessary to row quite short strokes.

Towards the end of the stroke the arms are bent and this helps the oarsman to come upright. It's best to keep the elbows in and good rowers display no flamboyance. They seem to be almost lazy and they can go on for hours without getting a stitch or without breathing heavily.

The blades should be slightly angled, with the top edge just a little forward of the vertical, when in the water. This keeps the blade submerged and stops any tendency of the oars to lift out of the rowlocks. If the oars insist on jumping out, the fault is almost always the rower's, but the best thing is to tie them in – not too tight or this will hamper easy rowing. When the oarsman gets expert, the oars will stop wanting to lift out and the lashing can be forgotten.

Practice is everything. It takes the grind out of the job, gets results and, little by little, a rower wonders why he did not become expert long ago. Feathering makes double sense; it reduces windage and if a blade touches the sea surface on the return stroke it will ski off, causing no splash and virtually no resistance. If the wind is fresh from astern and there is no sea, feathering is stopped to get as much help from the breeze as possible. But who rows under such conditions?

Dinghies over about 14 ft (4.3 m) can be rowed by two people sitting on the midships thwart together. It takes practice and if one member of the crew is a complete beginner, the other should put a hand on both oars so that they are swung in perfect unison. For a long row it is almost always best for the two members of the crew to take turn and turn about, rather than row together. Only when a short ferocious burst of speed is needed, perhaps to get up-tide to a mooring, or to get out of a fairway when fog suddenly comes down, is it best to row two together.

The person not rowing will normally steer, but on all other occasions the rudder should be removed and the centreplate taken up fully.

Types of Oars

The longest possible oars are best, so far as rowing is concerned. The limitation is usually the space available for stowing them. Even if they are lashed down partly on the foredeck, partly on the forward ends of the side decks, they are obtrusive. It is important that they never protrude outboard when stowed.

Spoon-bladed oars give better performance than flat bladed ones, but they cost a lot more and they tend to be less rugged. To reduce chipping and to cure chipped blades I use fibreglass bandaging with epoxy resin. It stands up to rough usage and it is easy to renew every few months or years. I have also bound the looms of oars with the same bandaging to strengthen them. This must be done before leathering. There are plastic substitutes for leathering, but they have a fixed internal diameter so they cannot be slid over an oar which has been thickened up, and they are slippery so the oars slide inboard and outwards too easily. Experienced oarsmen keep coming back to traditional leather.

Apart from giving an oar extra strength, the thickening, if properly designed, also adds weight to the inboard end to make rowing easier. Some oarsmen add lead to the inner end of the oars to make them balance almost perfectly so that, when the handles have to be depressed to lift the blades out of the water, little effort is needed. The neatest way of doing this is to drill a longitudinal hole in the end of each handle and pour lead in. If the holes go more than three-quarters of the way down the handle, they will cause weakness at that highly stressed point where the handle joins the loom.

Almost always the leathering is nailed in place with copper tacks. This is poor practice because the nail holes occur at the place where the oar is most likely to break. A better scheme is to lace the leathers on, using leather thongs which should be upwards when rowing, but which can stand the rough treatment if they happen to be down in the crutch of the rowlock for a few hours' hard work. In any case the leathers should be greased with lanoline or vaseline.

Leather can be hard to get but some shoe repairers as well as some sailmakers supply it. Alternatively, a tough, man-made rope, such as ⅛ in (3 mm) diameter Terylene (Dacron), can be used, though it will not last as long as leathering. An observant crew will notice it is wearing through and will renew it, but this is inconvenient in the middle of a holiday. It is best if secured with epoxy resin.

The oars themselves are usually made of spruce or one of its near cousins, but for tough oars ash is the traditional material. Before buying or using an oar it should be inspected for splits and faults. Knots which are less than ½ in (12 mm) diameter are acceptable in the blade, but otherwise the grain must be perfect.

Paddles

Various small plastic paddles are available from chandlers. They are, in effect, scoops held in the hand and used for short distances. The paddler's arm acts as the 'loom' or 'shank' of the paddle, so in anything but the calmest weather he gets wet. But then this sort of demi-paddle can only be used for limited periods and in settled conditions. They are seldom seen on cruising craft and then only on the smallest open boats.

Ordinary single paddles, as sold by chandlers, are designed for canoes, so they are too short for use in most sailing dinghies. Canoe paddles are usually available in lengths of 3 ft 4 in (1 m) and 4 ft (1.2 m) but neither of these sizes is usually long enough for us and, of course, there is no way anyone can use the kayak double-ended paddle in a sailing dinghy.

As paddling is usually done by sitting on the side deck, a long paddle is needed. I've used an ordinary 6 ft (2 m) oar effectively. Its length gives a powerful stroke and the blade is easily immersed well ahead of the paddler. If one person paddles the other will probably steer. If both paddle – and this makes sense since it is a good use of the available 'horsepower' – one will probably sit slightly forward of amidships on one side and one slightly aft on the other. I'm told that left-handed people like to paddle on one side and right-handed people on the other, but this sort of temperamental attitude is more suitable for amateur dramatics or tennis and finds little sympathy in my boats.

Paddling is hard work but one advantage is that the operator is facing the way he is going, unlike rowing. It is awkward work in rough conditions and in anything except a flat calm it is easy to splash water into the boat. Even experienced people find it hard to keep paddling non-stop for half an hour and if there is a lot of mileage to cover, it makes sense to change sides every so often, or take it in turns to paddle.

The crew should dispose their weight so that the transom is not immersed and causing drag in the water. The same applies when rowing, of course.

A light paddle is needed since it has to be lifted out of the water about 1,000 times every hour. So anyone who has to go long distances is well advised to make or buy light paddles with all surplus thickness shaved off the blade. Traditionally, the blade

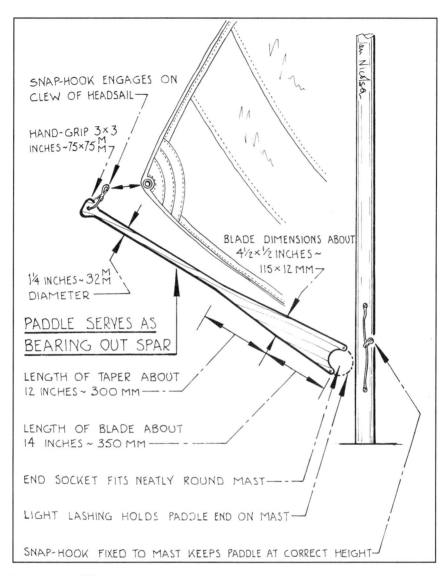

SNAP-HOOK ENGAGES ON CLEW OF HEADSAIL⌐

HAND-GRIP 3×3 INCHES~75×75 M M⌐

BLADE DIMENSIONS ABOUT 4½×½ INCHES ~ 115×12 MM⌐

1¼ INCHES~32 M M DIAMETER

PADDLE SERVES AS BEARING OUT SPAR

LENGTH OF TAPER ABOUT 12 INCHES ~ 300 MM

LENGTH OF BLADE ABOUT 14 INCHES ~ 350 MM

END SOCKET FITS NEATLY ROUND MAST

LIGHT LASHING HOLDS PADDLE END ON MAST

SNAP-HOOK FIXED TO MAST KEEPS PADDLE AT CORRECT HEIGHT

Dual-purpose paddle

When the wind dies some boats are rowed, but oars take up a lot of space on board. Paddles take up less room and are adequate for short spells of manpower/womanpower. A paddle can also be used to wing out the headsail when running downwind. The blade end needs shaping to fit round the mast, and the handle end must have a device to attach to the headsail clew.

is oval, not rectangular in elevation, with the sides of the blade thinned to perhaps less than ⅛ in (3 mm). The shaft must be easily grasped, so small people need small paddles. The parts held must be absolutely smooth and pleasant to grasp – even then plenty of blisters will be generated. Clear-grained fault-free spruce is an excellent material for paddles. It may be strengthened with 'hi-tech' material such as carbon fibre for people who like that sort of thing.

Where the shaft is gripped the diameter should be 1 ¼ in (32 mm) for the man who has a typical hand span of 8 ¾ in (220 mm). Many people like a shaft top in the form of a flat-topped triangle 3 in × 3 in (75 mm × 75 mm). This triangular top is typically ½ in (12 mm) thick with well-rounded corners and edges. It tapers into the shaft, as does the blade.

Paddles may be made up of aluminium tube with blades of the same material or wood. Both ends of the shaft must be plugged to ensure the paddle floats. As with so much gear, it is essential to have sea trials in tough conditions to make sure that the paddles do not break when stressed. The old rule, 'If it bends enough to make anyone cringe, it's too light' applies here, as elsewhere.

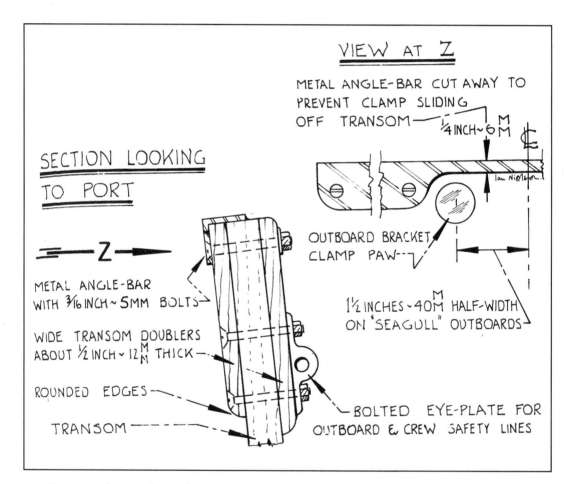

Transom changes for outboard engines

The typical cruising dinghy does not have a transom which is designed to take an outboard. The stern needs stiffening and there needs to be some form of padding to protect the structure from crushing by the engine clamps. Guard pieces are bolted on the inboard and outboard faces, with waterproof bedding underneath. The top metal angle-bar shown here not only stiffens the transom, it also prevents the engine being lost overboard if the clamps are not tight enough and slip upwards on the transom.

Outboard Engines as Auxiliary Power

For when the wind disappears there is nothing handier than a light, quiet outboard to ease the boat along. The only trouble is that only electric outboards are quiet and they have a very limited range between battery recharge so they are seldom suitable except on inland waters. Small petrol outboards can be rattly, not very reliable, and they use a lot of fuel for every ten miles travelled.

It is not surprising that many open-boat sailors prefer to wait for the wind and tide, rather than carry a sharp-cornered, smelly, oily lump of machinery which takes up a lot of space in the boat. Those of us who do use outboards, and have done so for years, know that there are basic rules:

1. Even with care, outboards do not last long. Besides, less than one in 1,000 gets adequate care.
2. It's rare to get more than six years' use from an outboard, but the fault lies almost always with the owner who does not take enough trouble over the engine.
3. The lighter, and therefore handier, an engine, the less reliable it is, and the more full of delicate parts.
4. Good seamanship, when applied to outboards, or indeed any gear, consists of taking precautions. So tie the engine down in its locker and tie it onto a strong point before clamping it onto the transom.

My outboard has a length of ⅜ in (10 mm) diameter rope spliced round the shaft near the top and this is used for lashing it in its locker. Before the engine is lifted onto the transom this rope, which is 6 ft (2 m) long, is securely knotted round a thwart. Then, when the greasy engine slips through the cold fingers and plunges overboard, at least the crisis is limited. Even when an engine is apparently tightly clamped onto the transom, it may vibrate loose.

The clamps must be tight, so they usually gouge deep into wood. In one way this is good because the jaws of the clamp often bite so deep there is only a limited chance that the engine will shake itself overboard. But it does the wood of the transom a lot of harm. To avoid this there should be double pads, typically 16 in × 8 in × ¾ in (400 mm × 200 mm × 20 mm) inside and outside the transom to spread the load and to absorb the crushing of the clamps. These pads are held by four 3⁄16 in (4 mm) bolts, so every couple of years it is easy to renew the pads, which should be of hardwood.

Because the outboard is only needed when there is no wind or rough sea, its horsepower can be minimal, provided there is no strong tide to overcome. For boats up to about 12 ft (3.7 m) 3 hp should be ample and 2 might do unless the boat is heavily laden. Boats up to about 15 ft (4.5 m) need a 5 hp engine, though 4 will do for anyone not in a hurry. Around 8 hp is needed for a boat in the 18 to 30 ft (5.5 to 6 m) range.

As one fit, tough man cannot keep up a rowing rate of even 1 hp for more than a few minutes, it is obvious that an outboard is far better than rowing if there is a serious distance to travel. However, a man needs only a little food and seldom spare parts.

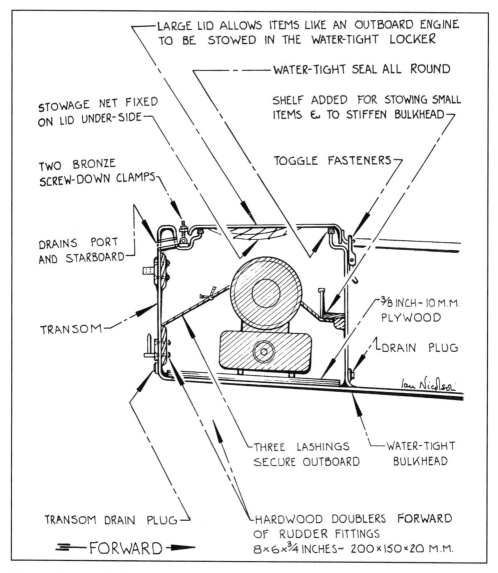

LARGE LID ALLOWS ITEMS LIKE AN OUTBOARD ENGINE TO BE STOWED IN THE WATER-TIGHT LOCKER

WATER-TIGHT SEAL ALL ROUND

STOWAGE NET FIXED ON LID UNDER-SIDE

SHELF ADDED FOR STOWING SMALL ITEMS & TO STIFFEN BULKHEAD

TWO BRONZE SCREW-DOWN CLAMPS

TOGGLE FASTENERS

DRAINS PORT AND STARBOARD

$^{3}/_{8}$ INCH ~ 10 M.M. PLYWOOD

TRANSOM

DRAIN PLUG

Ian Nicolson

THREE LASHINGS SECURE OUTBOARD

WATER-TIGHT BULKHEAD

TRANSOM DRAIN PLUG

HARDWOOD DOUBLERS FORWARD OF RUDDER FITTINGS 8×6×$^{3}/_{4}$ INCHES ~ 200×150×20 M.M.

FORWARD

Watertight stem locker

This view looking to port, shows the standard stern locker of the 14 ft Wanderer class cruising dinghy, with some additions. That shelf with its high fiddle is ideal for stowing gear like spare sparking plugs for the engine, because such items must be kept out of the bilge.

The net secured under the lid is handy for books and charts. The plywood doubler on the bottom is needed to prevent the engine damaging the hull, and the lashing lines are secured under the fillet piece of the shelf, also under the extra large rudder fitting pads.

If an outboard is carried, an instruction book and a set of basic spares, such as starter cord, plugs and spanner ('wrench' in America) are needed. Many outboards have a device such as a shear pin which is intended to break when the propeller hits a solid obstruction. This protects the prop but spares of the shear pin are needed on board, not lying at home in a drawer.

Spare fuel should be carried in a container which has a totally leak-proof cap. The best containers are not made of steel (because this rusts within a month) and they have screw-on flexible tubes which fit where the filler cap goes. When refuelling the end of this flexible pipe is pushed right into the engine's tank, so there is no spillage and no waste. Trying to refuel an engine which is clamped onto the transom, using a fuel funnel, is a smelly, mucky job which ends up with spilt fuel spread across the ocean. In heavy rain lots of fresh water joins the petrol in the tank, because the funnel acts as a scoop.

When buying an engine it seldom pays to go for the one which is lightest for a given horsepower. Lightness is often achieved at the expense of reliability and ruggedness.

Whichever engine is used, it is worth fending off the worst attacks on it. The top should be dried off after use and wrapped in a waterproof cover. If this cover is put on when the engine is wet, moisture is trapped round the working parts and corrosion is even faster than usual. The electrical parts are the weak link in these engines, so it is sensible to replace them if the engine seems to be getting lazy. After half a season's regular use it is a good idea to renew the plug and its connecting cable.

The fuel filter should be cleaned monthly and, if it seems to be collecting a lot of dirt, the fuel tank and cans for spare petrol should be rinsed out. If this produces a lot of what might be rust chips, it is time to renew the container.

When the propeller gets sad looking either have it repaired or get a new one and keep the old as a spare.

Our engine, when not in use, has a specially made PVC bag tied on the bottom end to protect the propeller and adjacent parts. This bag is padded and has a wood base like those traditional canvas buckets which yachtsmen used sixty years ago. A local sail maker will stitch up a bag like this and another bag to go over the top of the engine, if you coax him carefully during his slack season in the autumn or winter.

CHAPTER 7

Cruising Grounds

A small open boat can voyage wherever there is sufficient water to float her. She can be conveniently moved to new cruising grounds, rowed behind or loaded on top of a car. She can be sent by rail, by sea and even by air.

Only weather conditions, fierce tides and absence of sheltered waters will make an experienced owner hesitate before exploring a new area.

Beginners must start in well protected waters, then progress to semi-sheltered conditions, before going on short coastal passages in settled weather.

Inexperienced crews need quite narrow rivers and creeks, not much more than two or three hundred yards wide, so that the sea cannot get rough in the confines of the channels. If a boat gets into difficulties, there is help or at least a friendly shore not far away. Apart from its overcrowding, the Norfolk Broads is probably one ideal place in Britain. Admittedly, it can be necessary to beat for a long way up a narrow river, and if the jib is not self-tacking this can be hard work. But if there is ample wind the jib may be dropped and the boat sailed under main only. Probably the best approach is to change the destination and sail downwind!

The condition of the sea and wave height are important, even for very experienced crews. Wherever the proposed cruise is to take place, the important consideration is the distance between the land to windward and the point where the boat is sailing. It is broadly true that the waves will never be more than 2 ft high if the land is less than 1 mile upwind. This limit applies even if the wind is blowing hard, or has been blowing from that direction for days. These factors affect the sea conditions further offshore.

Ten miles offshore, the waves will be about 5 ft high, which is fine if they are not white-capped, but the chances of them breaking dangerously are much greater.

In non-tidal areas waves of 2 ft and less are unlikely to break seriously until the wind is far above the force which suits small boats. So as a broad generalisation, river estuaries, natural harbours, inlets, lochs and fiords less than 2 miles wide, or long, are good for cruising, even when the crew are only moderately experienced. There are plenty of exceptions. I've been reaching down a Scottish loch with the land well under half-a-mile to windward, when gusts have come down the mountain, apparently at an angle to the horizontal, as if the wind were driving arrow-like into the sea's surface instead of along it. One minute the boat was cruising comfortably, under rather short canvas, and the next there was a lot of unwanted water sloshing inboard, and we were letting the sheets run out in a flurry.

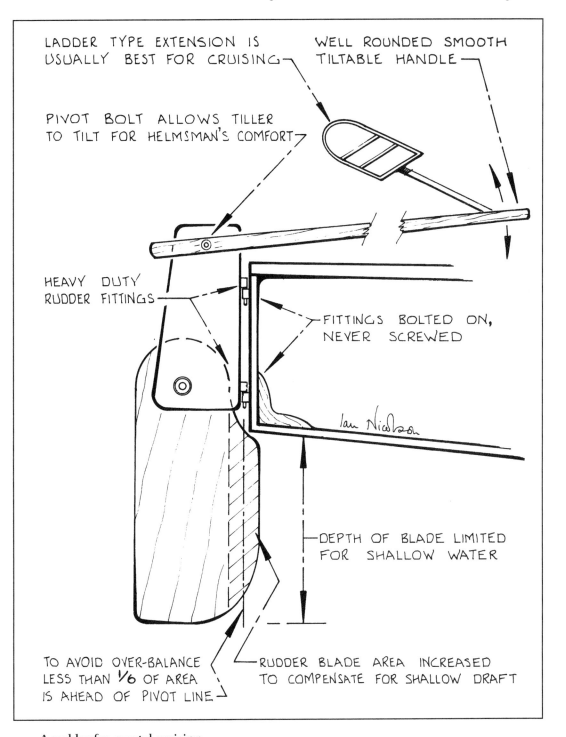

LADDER TYPE EXTENSION IS USUALLY BEST FOR CRUISING

WELL ROUNDED SMOOTH TILTABLE HANDLE

PIVOT BOLT ALLOWS TILLER TO TILT FOR HELMSMAN'S COMFORT

HEAVY DUTY RUDDER FITTINGS

FITTINGS BOLTED ON, NEVER SCREWED

Ian Nicolson

DEPTH OF BLADE LIMITED FOR SHALLOW WATER

TO AVOID OVER-BALANCE LESS THAN 1/6 OF AREA IS AHEAD OF PIVOT LINE

RUDDER BLADE AREA INCREASED TO COMPENSATE FOR SHALLOW DRAFT

A rudder for coastal cruising

Even a pivoting rudder which can be lifted is not ideal for working close inshore. The best type has a relatively broad, shallow blade, so that it can be kept fully down in all but the shallowest water. To minimise weather helm it often helps to have some of the blade area ahead of the pivot point.

The rule about waterways being moderately safe if they are less than 2 miles across (in any direction) therefore needs modification. If the adjacent ground is high, dangerous gusting can occur. If the tides are moderate, let alone strong, then sea conditions can be bad. What constitutes a 'moderate' tide is arguable, but any tide over 2 knots seems strong when it runs against a fresh breeze.

When cruising most people will not want to be under way for more than eight hours each day and, at an average of 3 knots, that gives a range of 24 miles. If the winds are light, or from ahead, and the tide adverse, it can be difficult to cover more than 12 miles, especially if the dinghy is a small one, or well laden. So a cruising ground can be quite small and still interesting and enjoyable.

Areas like Poole Harbour, Chichester Harbour, Falmouth, Plymouth and Milford Haven are all large enough for a long weekend's cruise, with a diversity of destinations for each night's halt.

With a few weekends' practice most crews will get confident and have enough experience to go further afield. When they feel they can cope with winds up to Force 5, even with a rough wind-against-tide sea, they can try semi-sheltered waters. Best known of these in Britain is the stretch between Chichester and Keyhaven, the Solent-Spithead area. Other areas are the Clyde and the Essex rivers.

The next stage is to make coastal passages, taking proper care to listen to weather forecasts and to avoid risky places such as tidal races off headlands.

Cruising Grounds in the UK

Crews who can make safe passages in open waters will seldom want to go along the coast non-stop just for the fun of it. Most will enjoy a region where there are harbours every 10 or, at most, 15 mile intervals. The English South and East Coasts are ideal, especially as there tend to be plenty of harbours big enough for a day's adventuring if the weather outside is rough. The Devon and Cornish south coast is ideal because such inlets as Dartmouth, Salcombe and the Yealm River have spacious stretches of sheltered waters which cannot be explored in just an hour. The same applies to the coast from the mouth of the Thames northwards as far as Harwich.

The West Coast of Scotland from the Clyde northwards is a series of semi-sheltered areas. The disadvantages hereabouts are:

1. Shores tend to be rocky so that beaching needs care and slipways are few.
2. The average rainfall is higher than the rest of Britain. The best time to avoid rain is the end of May and the beginning of June, when there is a good chance of getting easterly winds which tend to be below Force 4 and are in any case off the shore. It may be a bit chilly.
3. Much of the coast is relatively deserted, so if a boat gets into trouble, she may not be seen.
4. Facilities are available, but not in the profusion found in areas like the English South Coast.

On the other hand:

a) The scenery is unrivalled.
b) There is no crowding and ample space everywhere.
c) Being rocky, it is normally possible to sail close to the shore.
d) The area is well charted and supplied with navigation books. The Clyde Cruising Club (address Suite 101, The Pentagon Centre, 36 Washington Street, Glasgow, Scotland, G3 8AZ) issues superb pilotage books which list the hundreds of inlets and anchorages.

The Scottish coasts favour big dinghies and a boat of 15 ft or more is recommended. The East Coast of Scotland is suitable for experienced people. In most years by the end of June the prevailing wind has gone to the west, so it is off the shore and this gives a relatively calm sea. Many of the harbours dry out and there are plenty of stretches of sandy beach. South of the Firth of Forth the coast is becoming more popular, but it is still relatively unspoilt and quiet.

Some of the inland Scottish lochs, like Loch Lomond and Loch Awe, are big enough to be interesting and give a long weekend's cruising and a different anchorage each night, as well as a chance to catch fish.

European Cruising

All around Europe there are places where the crew of an open boat can enjoy cruising. The North Coast of France tends to be tougher than the South Coast of England because the tides are stronger, also the harbours are less sheltered and many dry out at least partially at low water. But the Morbihan, on the Atlantic Coast, has been compared with Poole Harbour.

Holland has much to recommend it in that there are so many miles of inland waterways, but these favour powerboats rather than sailing craft.

Scandinavia, especially Denmark, has ample sheltered and semi-sheltered water, though the locals tend to sail mostly in June, July and August, but not so much outside those months, suggesting the weather suits this limited period.

The Mediterranean is not ideal for sailing dinghies designed for cruising because there is often too much or too little wind. But for the person who wants to go a-roving in an open powerboat, this sea has a lot to commend it. The growing sport of cruising in inflatable dinghies, sometimes with very powerful outboards, seems to have been born in the Eastern Med. and is understandably popular there.

North America

For an experienced crew, the East and West Coasts of Canada have miles of suitable waters, but conditions here are less suitable for beginners, except well inland and in settled weather.

The US East Coast has some interesting areas. For an experienced owner Long Island Sound has much to offer and parts of Chesapeake Bay are even better, being suitable for beginners as well as practised open-boat sailers.

One way to select a new region is to get out an atlas and find a length of coast which is protected by one or more off-lying islands, or which has a large enclosed bay, or a

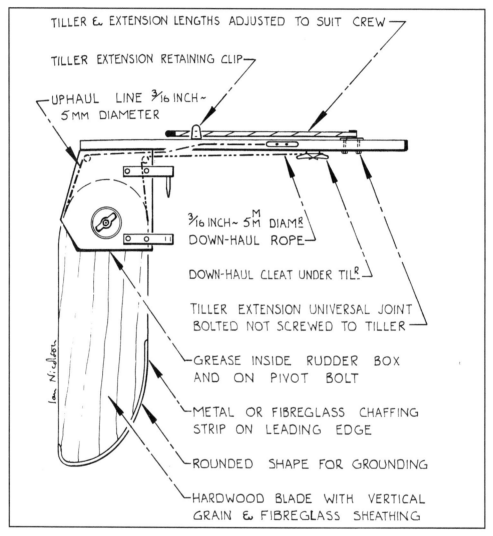

TILLER & EXTENSION LENGTHS ADJUSTED TO SUIT CREW

TILLER EXTENSION RETAINING CLIP

UPHAUL LINE ³⁄₁₆ INCH ~ 5 MM DIAMETER

³⁄₁₆ INCH ~ 5 M DIAM^M DOWN-HAUL ROPE

DOWN-HAUL CLEAT UNDER TIL^R

TILLER EXTENSION UNIVERSAL JOINT BOLTED NOT SCREWED TO TILLER

GREASE INSIDE RUDDER BOX AND ON PIVOT BOLT

METAL OR FIBREGLASS CHAFFING STRIP ON LEADING EDGE

ROUNDED SHAPE FOR GROUNDING

HARDWOOD BLADE WITH VERTICAL GRAIN & FIBREGLASS SHEATHING

Drop rudder

A lifting rudder blade is essential for almost all cruising, but especially when coming ashore on a shelving beach. The blade must be easy to lift and lower in all circumstances, and a pair of simple two-part tackles may be needed even on a 12 ft boat, especially if the inside of the box is not kept greased.

After perhaps half a season's use, the chaffing strip on the leading edge may need repairing or renewing, but it does protect the blade.

Both up-haul and down-haul lines must be fixed with at least three 12-gauge 1 in (25 mm) screws into the rudder blade.

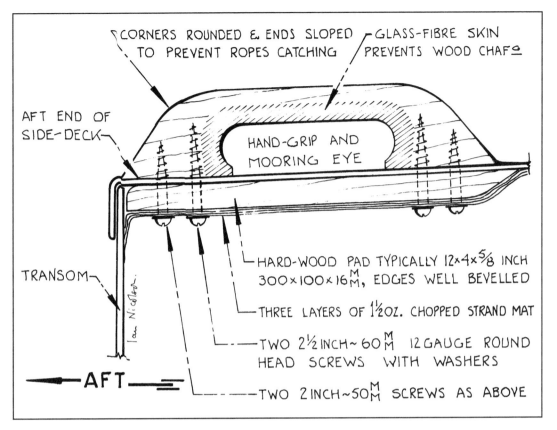

CORNERS ROUNDED & ENDS SLOPED TO PREVENT ROPES CATCHING

GLASS-FIBRE SKIN PREVENTS WOOD CHAFE

AFT END OF SIDE-DECK

HAND-GRIP AND MOORING EYE

TRANSOM

AFT

HARD-WOOD PAD TYPICALLY 12×4×⅝ INCH 300×100×16 MM, EDGES WELL BEVELLED

THREE LAYERS OF 1½OZ. CHOPPED STRAND MAT

TWO 2½ INCH ~ 60 MM 12 GAUGE ROUND HEAD SCREWS WITH WASHERS

TWO 2 INCH ~50 MM SCREWS AS ABOVE

Aft carrying handle and mooring strongpoint

This handle has all sorts of uses apart from being ideal when the boat is being carried up a beach, or tied alongside in harbour. It is good for taking the lashings which hold the boat onto a trailer, can be used to hold the outboard engine safety line, or the crew's personal lifelines, and it is a good aft fixing point for a tent, and so on.

section of coast riddled with numerous deep inlets. Next, write off for a yachtsman's guide to the area. If there is no such guide, it must be concluded that the area is either unsuitable for sailing or is remote, undeveloped and short of facilities. For the adventurous these conditions can be an enormous attraction. Beginners should stay away from such places until they are well practised and totally self-reliant.

Books and Information

Pilot books covering different areas, written specially for sailing people, are sold by:

Adlard Coles Nautical

Imray

Stanford Maritime,

Many of these pilot books are available in libraries and, since books get wet and often ruined afloat, it may be a good idea to photostat only the pages needed for a voyage and take these afloat. They can be sprayed with a waterproofing compound to keep them from going soggy when conditions get tough.

In good major libraries in capitals and large cities there will be copies of the official pilotage books for every ocean of the world.

These are worth studying and there is some useful information in them, but they are so heavily angled towards helping the officers of big ships that many of the paragraphs will be misleading or incorrect for small boats.

If a pilot book for a particular area is not available in a local library, the librarian will arrange for one to be borrowed from another library if an application form is filled in. Sometimes this form has to be sent to different libraries before the correct book is found, so several weeks have to be allowed for this search.

Before going to a new area a lot of information can be gleaned from tourist centres, though this is usually more helpful to land-bound travellers. In most countries the information is available by writing to The Tourist Information Centre of the appropriate local town. Such places are good at supplying lists of small hotels as well as bed-and-breakfast houses, which are useful if the weather is vile, or when the crew need a break from the rigours of living in a very small boat. A detailed letter from a boat owner may bring a reply with data about launching sites and boatyards.

To obtain information from other countries, it is only necessary to write to the correct embassy and hint that a visit to their delightful country may be in the offing. This often results in a deluge of pamphlets and leaflets extolling the virtues of all the delectable regions in their country. A letter asking for specific information about such matters as launching slipways, import duties on boats brought in for a limited period, the availability of yacht repair yards and so on, should be sent well in advance of a visit. Such inquiries are liable to be forwarded to the central yachting authority, which in turn may have to forward them to a specific regional organisation. All this takes time.

Specific information can be obtained direct from the central yachting authority of any of the main maritime countries. In Britain this is:

Royal Yachting Association.

To learn about boatyards, marinas and commercial organisations in a particular district in Britain, inquiries should be made to:

British Marine Industries Federation.

Even the best equipped and most carefully sailed boat may need running repairs which the crew cannot do unaided. Or the available holiday period may end before the boat reaches the port where the cruise was intended to end. For such reasons it is advisable to know where the boat may be left in safe hands until the owner can come back to sail her home, or collect her with car and trailer.

An organisation in Britain which has a widespread network of boat-minders and yacht yards ready to cater for members is the Cruising Association of Ivory House, St Katherine's Dock, London, E1 9AT. In many respects this is the ideal club for anyone who shifts his sailing ground year by year, or even several times each year.

Anyone planning far-ranging cruising will find the Ocean Cruising Club's unique system of worldwide Port Officers a great help. The only snag is that to become a member it is necessary to sail a voyage of 1,000 miles between harbours. One cannot go round and round the local racing circuit 400 times to get into this club.

Insurance

Before setting out to a new region, the insurance policy should be checked. Some policies cover a limited area and some insurance companies will not insure boats in certain waters, or will only do so if the premium is raised. The cruising districts which attract these extra costs are not necessarily dangerous; it is just that the underwriters have found they have more claims from them. These claims may arise because the moorings are exposed and the local cruising may not be extra hazardous. However, high premia should be taken as a warning.

It can be difficult to get insurance in one country for cruising in a far-away place. The best move then is to get insurance through a broker who lives and works near the proposed cruising ground. For instance, any European owner who plans to sail in America will find it hard to get insurance from a broker near home, but probably not hard from an American one. For very long offshore voyages insurance is often difficult or impossible to obtain.

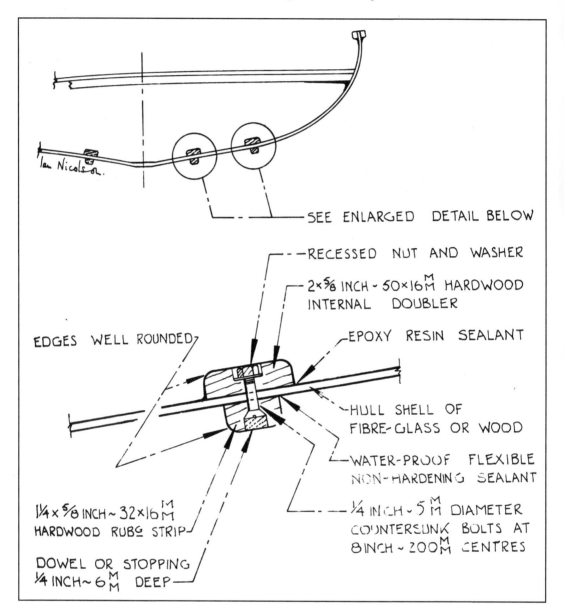

Ian Nicolson.

SEE ENLARGED DETAIL BELOW

- RECESSED NUT AND WASHER

2×⅝ INCH ~ 50×16M HARDWOOD
INTERNAL   DOUBLER

EDGES WELL ROUNDED

EPOXY RESIN SEALANT

HULL SHELL OF
FIBRE-GLASS OR WOOD

WATER-PROOF FLEXIBLE
NON-HARDENING SEALANT

1¼ × ⅝ INCH ~ 32×16M
HARDWOOD RUBS STRIP

¼ INCH ~ 5M DIAMETER
COUNTERSUNK BOLTS AT
8 INCH ~ 200M CENTRES

DOWEL OR STOPPING
¼ INCH ~ 6M DEEP

Hull protection

Cruising so often involves hauling the boat up a rough beach, or running aground. To protect the hull, whatever it is made of, wood rubbing strips are hard to beat. They are light and cheap, they are easy to make and replace, they cause no corrosion and they often strengthen the hull.

The inboard strips may have to be made extra wide, to act as floorboards, or to give the crew a good foot grip.

CHAPTER 8

Planning a Cruise

Look at the log of an old sailing ship and it will be seen that the heading reads:

FROM: Here the port of departure is named.
TOWARDS: And here the Captain notes the port he hopes to reach.

The important word is 'Towards' because there is nothing so uncertain as voyaging in small vessels, especially when wind is the motive power. This means that any plan for a voyage should be as flexible as possible. The ideal holiday starts from a central position from which it is possible to sail in three or four widespread directions. Then, if the wind is westerly, the course can be easterly, or perhaps even better, north-east or south-east. Even if it is north or south, it will mean that the boat is reaching, so performance will be encouraging.

The best departure points also have some well-sheltered waters nearby, perhaps a narrow river or winding inlet, so that if the weather is too windy for coastal cruising, the first day or two can be spent exploring the immediate locality. When it is not possible to start from a harbour offering alternative cruises, a good plan is to have a flexible starting date. Then the weather maps can be watched day by day until it is reasonably certain that the required winds are likely to be blowing, for the start of the cruise. Naturally, this only suits people who can take time off as required. (There are people who take jobs to suit their cruising, such as school teachers who get long holidays. This is 'advanced planning' on a grand scale.)

In certain areas prevailing winds live up to their name and blow consistently from one direction, which makes planning easier. However, it may also mean that getting back after sailing downwind during the beginning of the cruise can only be accomplished by a long beat, or by using the trailer. To find out about the consistency of prevailing winds the appropriate pilot books or the hydrographic charts should be studied.

Predicting how far a small boat can travel within a given time is a risky business. The toughness and experience of the crew, the standard and tuning of the dinghy, the influence of the tide and, above all, the direction and strength of the wind are all critical.

Under ideal conditions it is possible to cover more than 130 miles in twenty-four hours. This calls for a very high level of luck, skill and determination, also a well fitted out fast boat. In light headwinds the crew may still be keen and experienced and only cover 100 miles in a week of persistent trying. So sensible planning assumes a very wide range of weekly mileages; it also works on the basis that potential stopping places should, where possible, be no more than 10 miles apart.

For this sort of broad planning plenty of charts are needed and these are costly. Some people share charts, and in a few areas they can be hired. If the terrain is rocky, they do not get out of date fast, so a chart which is regularly updated lasts for years.

If a chart is much used all summer in an open boat, it is likely to be worn out well before autumn. I've come ashore on more than one occasion with charts ruined by one hectic weekend's sailing, in spite of the care we try to take over our navigation equipment.

A triangular section tent has less room inside than one with ample width at the top, but it is easier to rig, to stow, and it costs less, besides presenting less windage. This is the 16-foot Carra with outboard secured well clear of the rudder.

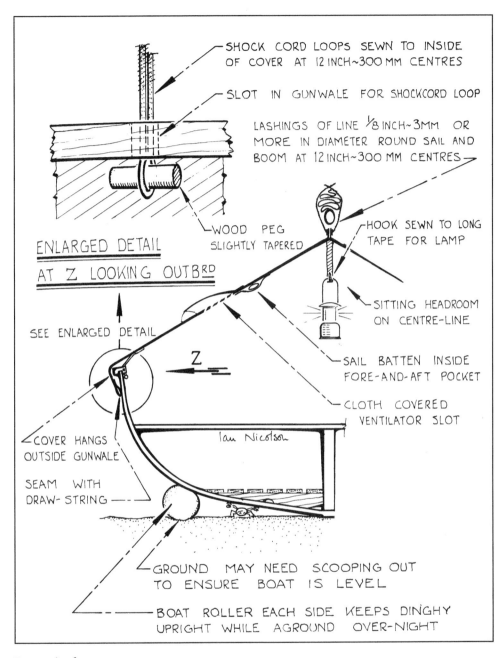

SHOCK CORD LOOPS SEWN TO INSIDE OF COVER AT 12 INCH~300 MM CENTRES

SLOT IN GUNWALE FOR SHOCKCORD LOOP

LASHINGS OF LINE ⅛ INCH~3MM OR MORE IN DIAMETER ROUND SAIL AND BOOM AT 12 INCH~300 MM CENTRES

HOOK SEWN TO LONG TAPE FOR LAMP

WOOD PEG SLIGHTLY TAPERED

ENLARGED DETAIL AT Z LOOKING OUTBRD

SEE ENLARGED DETAIL

SITTING HEADROOM ON CENTRE-LINE

Z

SAIL BATTEN INSIDE FORE-AND-AFT POCKET

CLOTH COVERED VENTILATOR SLOT

Ian Nicolson

COVER HANGS OUTSIDE GUNWALE

SEAM WITH DRAW-STRING

GROUND MAY NEED SCOOPING OUT TO ENSURE BOAT IS LEVEL

BOAT ROLLER EACH SIDE KEEPS DINGHY UPRIGHT WHILE AGROUND OVER-NIGHT

Low-price boat tent

A tent should be under the boom otherwise drips from the wet sail will fall on the crew. The simplest, cheapest tent shape is shown here, but it does not have much room beneath. Its edge has a continuous seam with a tightening line threaded through, but to keep the tent sides tight down all round there are 10 in (250 mm) long loops of shock cord which pass through slots in the gunwhale and are held by pegs. This avoids the need for cleats or hooks which tend to catch on clothes.

The long tape with a hook on the end is handy for the lamp which should not be close under the tent if it is the kind which gets hot.

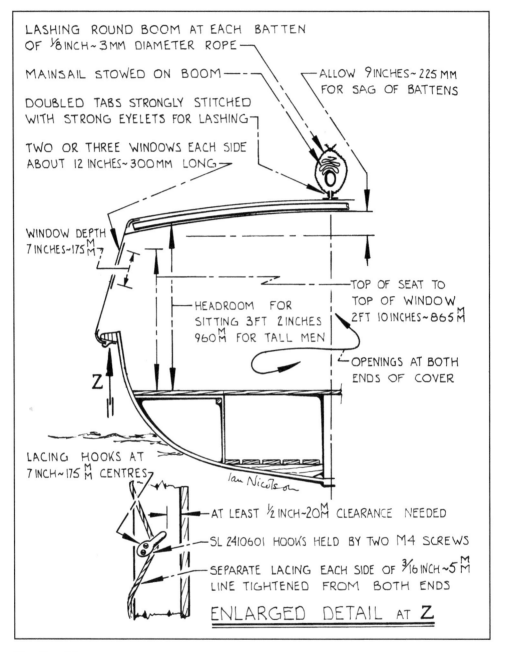

LASHING ROUND BOOM AT EACH BATTEN
OF ⅛INCH~3MM DIAMETER ROPE

MAINSAIL STOWED ON BOOM

DOUBLED TABS STRONGLY STITCHED
WITH STRONG EYELETS FOR LASHING

TWO OR THREE WINDOWS EACH SIDE
ABOUT 12 INCHES~300MM LONG

ALLOW 9INCHES~225MM
FOR SAG OF BATTENS

WINDOW DEPTH
7 INCHES~175 M M

HEADROOM FOR
SITTING 3FT 2INCHES
960M FOR TALL MEN

TOP OF SEAT TO
TOP OF WINDOW
2FT 10INCHES~865M M

OPENINGS AT BOTH
ENDS OF COVER

Z

LACING HOOKS AT
7 INCH~175 M M CENTRES

Ian Nicolson

AT LEAST ½INCH~20M M CLEARANCE NEEDED

SL 2410601 HOOKS HELD BY TWO M4 SCREWS

SEPARATE LACING EACH SIDE OF ³⁄₁₆INCH~5M M
LINE TIGHTENED FROM BOTH ENDS

ENLARGED DETAIL AT Z

Comfortable tent

If there is clear sitting headroom under a tent, right out to the sides, life aboard is easier than if
the crew have to do a lot of crouching. The crossbeams may be of alloy tube, plastic tube, heavy
sail batten material doubled or wood, including bamboo. Not shown are fore-and-aft stiffeners at
the top outer edge, because these will not be needed if there are crossbeams every 4 ft (1.2 m) or so.

The crossbeams slide into pockets which have doubled ends to deal with chafe. It is important
that the bottom edge of the sides is outside the gunwhale to prevent rain getting into the boat.
Windows are a luxury and are vulnerable, so they should be kept small to save money and
minimise the chances of damage.

Where tides run fast they usually dominate planning. There are plenty of occasions when a foul tide is strong enough to prevent any forward progress, especially if the wind is from ahead or is very light. Dealing with the tide can be fun or frustrating, according to the temperament and cunning of the crew. The trick is to make it a friend. When the tide runs your way, go with it.

But don't wait till it is running in the favourable direction. Get out into the adverse tide an hour before it is due to turn (unless it is exceptionally fast and the wind almost useless) and that way every moment of fair tide is used. In the same way, it is not always necessary to dodge out of the tide the moment it reverses.

A 'Wanderer' snugged down for the night with a full length wide high tent. There is a 'door' entrance just aft of the mast and a central slit at the transom.

Certainly, there are places where the tide seems to change direction 180 degrees in a few startling minutes. But in most places there is half an hour when the tide is trying to make up its mind and another mile or more may be snatched before the boat starts to lose ground.

It is not necessary to dodge into harbour to avoid a foul tide. Any sheltered bay will do and, if the wind is off the land, the boat can be anchored or even beached on an open, straight shore. For anyone trying to make a good mileage, the adverse tide time is used for sleeping and the boat hurried on, day or night, when the tide suits.

Long Cruises

If the cruise is a long one, it may be necessary to plan breaks, so that the crew can go back to work and return to the boat later. This may be by previous intention or it may be a technique used because a long spell of bad weather makes it sensible to interrupt the cruise. Of course, stormy weather can be used to sail on well-sheltered waters such as narrow rivers. So if the weather forecasts are discouraging just before or during a cruise, some enjoyable sailing is still possible if the boat can be diverted to go up a river. The other way to use time when the wind is too strong is to see the sights ashore, catch up on shopping and visiting a laundrette, and perhaps do some boat repairs. All these alternatives need pre-planning because laundrettes are not found in small villages, maintenance is easier if the boat is in a spacious, dry shed, and sightseeing such as visiting museums and art galleries is not easy out in the wilds. Of course, some people's idea of a relaxation from sailing is a mountain climb, but even that needs some planning; maps and walking boots must be taken on the boat or sent on ahead.

Planning an Overseas Cruise

If going abroad, preparatory work has to be started weeks, if not months, in advance. Passports and, where applicable, visas have to be obtained, as well as foreign currency and the appropriate documents for the boat. These vary from country to country and can change from one year to the next. The first move is to write to the embassy of the country concerned and give an outline of the proposed trip, type of boat, whether it will be sailed or trailed abroad, and so on. This will bring in reply a letter setting out all the current regulations and the letter itself should be put with the documents in a watertight bag and presented with the passports, etc. when arriving abroad. If the local officials say that this or that document is missing or incorrect, the letter is evidence that they are wrong. Locals sometimes have ideas which differ from the central government.

As a safety measure it is worth having extra documents; even in these so-called sophisticated times port officials are awed or at least mollified by a show of papers which look impressive. If going far, one should have a letter from the commodore of the home sailing club requesting one and all to render every help and assistance to the boat and crew. A Bill of Sale or a photostat of it, showing that the boat has been officially bought and duly paid for, is extra evidence. Some non-British owners use this form, especially if the boat was built or bought from Britain. A copy of the insurance policy is also worth carrying, as it too shows proof of ownership of the boat and can be a help if there is an accident and the boat requires repairs.

Most people carry money in the form of traveller's cheques and plastic cards. With credit and debit cards there are certain ones which can be more useful than others, and it is best to find out from a bank before going abroad which are best for particular countries. It is sensible to arrive with at least a little local money on board. Landfall may occur after the banks have closed for the night or weekend, or during some unexpected local holiday. If in doubt, American dollars are as near to a universal currency as anything except, of course, famous brands of Scotch whisky which have remarkable bartering powers.

Before departing, it is always advisable to clear customs, and when leaving some countries it is compulsory. When entering any country it is essential to clear customs and immigration and this can normally only be done at major or at least moderately large ports. It is generally essential to fly the yellow flag, requesting clearance, when visiting or returning from a foreign country. However, there are exceptions and it is best to get the current regulations from the authorities well before departing.

Clearing is done by visiting the customs house and it is advisable to write in advance and let the authorities know when you will be calling. On arrival sailing from a home part abroad the yellow 'Q' flag is flown from halfway up a shroud on a small boat, as this is the international signal that the yacht requests clearance. At the same time the owner's national flag should be flown from the stern and on dinghies it is often tied to the topping lift about 3 ft (1 m) above the boom, as very small craft seldom have flagstaffs or backstays.

A courtesy flag, which is the flag of the country being visited, is flown from below a crosstree or in the equivalent area. A word of warning here – nationalism takes many forms and currently some countries seem to take a delight in foxing the rest of the world by changing flags. This may be the result of a coup, or a shift of local sentiment, or a new alignment. What is all too common is that the old flag rouses local tempers and the innocent yachtsman may unwittingly cause trouble for himself by not keeping up to date with these changes.

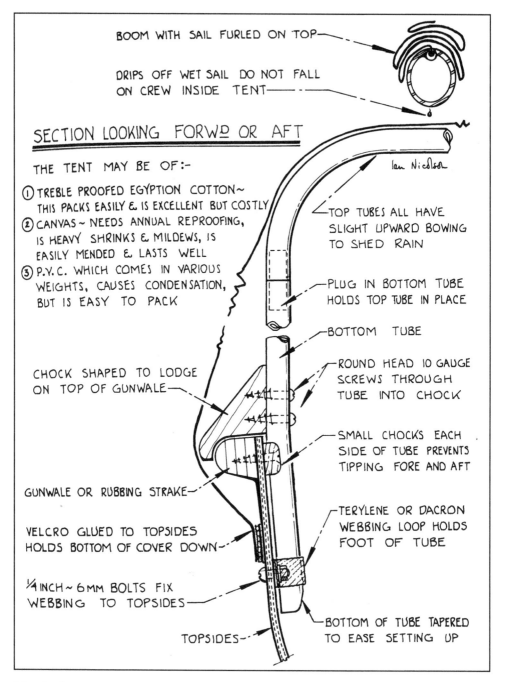

BOOM WITH SAIL FURLED ON TOP

DRIPS OFF WET SAIL DO NOT FALL ON CREW INSIDE TENT

SECTION LOOKING FORWᴰ OR AFT

Ian Nicolson

THE TENT MAY BE OF:-

① TREBLE PROOFED EGYPTION COTTON~ THIS PACKS EASILY & IS EXCELLENT BUT COSTLY

② CANVAS ~ NEEDS ANNUAL REPROOFING, IS HEAVY SHRINKS & MILDEWS, IS EASILY MENDED & LASTS WELL

③ P.V.C. WHICH COMES IN VARIOUS WEIGHTS, CAUSES CONDENSATION, BUT IS EASY TO PACK

TOP TUBES ALL HAVE SLIGHT UPWARD BOWING TO SHED RAIN

PLUG IN BOTTOM TUBE HOLDS TOP TUBE IN PLACE

BOTTOM TUBE

ROUND HEAD 10 GAUGE SCREWS THROUGH TUBE INTO CHOCK

CHOCK SHAPED TO LODGE ON TOP OF GUNWALE

SMALL CHOCKS EACH SIDE OF TUBE PREVENTS TIPPING FORE AND AFT

GUNWALE OR RUBBING STRAKE

VELCRO GLUED TO TOPSIDES HOLDS BOTTOM OF COVER DOWN

TERYLENE OR DACRON WEBBING LOOP HOLDS FOOT OF TUBE

¼ INCH ~ 6MM BOLTS FIX WEBBING TO TOPSIDES

TOPSIDES

BOTTOM OF TUBE TAPERED TO EASE SETTING UP

Metal tube tent supports

Each 'hoop' is in three parts, the two vertical or near vertical uprights, and the 'beam'. They are linked by wood, metal or plastic plugs which are fixed in the tops of the upright pieces, and are just the right diameter for the crosspieces. A push-fit join is needed here.

The uprights can be made gradually higher as they get near the aft end, to give extra headroom. This arrangement with the tent below the boom means that the crew do not have a wet sail dripping on them after they have set up the tent.

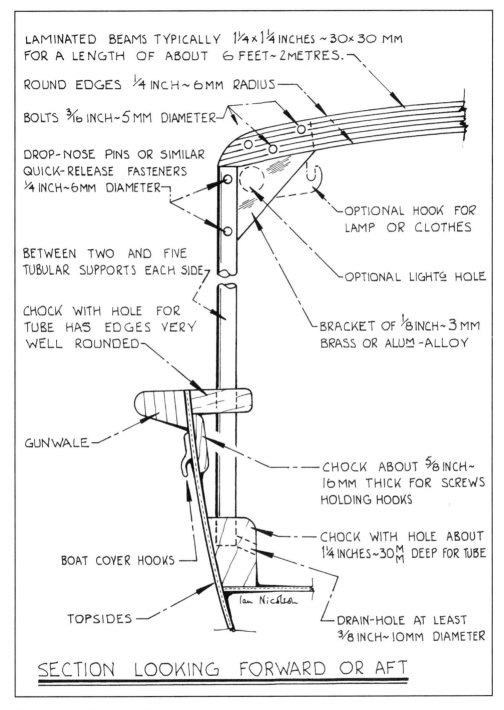

LAMINATED BEAMS TYPICALLY 1¼ x 1¼ INCHES ~ 30 x 30 MM
FOR A LENGTH OF ABOUT 6 FEET ~ 2 METRES.

ROUND EDGES ¼ INCH ~ 6 MM RADIUS

BOLTS ³⁄₁₆ INCH ~ 5 MM DIAMETER

DROP-NOSE PINS OR SIMILAR
QUICK-RELEASE FASTENERS
¼ INCH ~ 6 MM DIAMETER

OPTIONAL HOOK FOR
LAMP OR CLOTHES

OPTIONAL LIGHTS HOLE

BETWEEN TWO AND FIVE
TUBULAR SUPPORTS EACH SIDE

CHOCK WITH HOLE FOR
TUBE HAS EDGES VERY
WELL ROUNDED

BRACKET OF ⅛ INCH ~ 3 MM
BRASS OR ALUM-ALLOY

GUNWALE

CHOCK ABOUT ⅝ INCH ~
16 MM THICK FOR SCREWS
HOLDING HOOKS

CHOCK WITH HOLE ABOUT
1¼ INCHES ~ 30 ᴹᴹ DEEP FOR TUBE

BOAT COVER HOOKS

Ian Nicolson

TOPSIDES

DRAIN-HOLE AT LEAST
³⁄₈ INCH ~ 10 MM DIAMETER

SECTION LOOKING FORWARD OR AFT

Tent support framework

Metal tubes joined by crossbeams make a strong tent support, especially if the 'hoops' are spaced about 2 ft 6 in (750 mm) apart. These beams are detachable for stowing, and should have about 10 in (250 mm) of camber to shed rain. The chocks by the gunwhale and for the bottom of each tube are made as unobtrusive as possible and heavily rounded to avoid snagging oilskins.

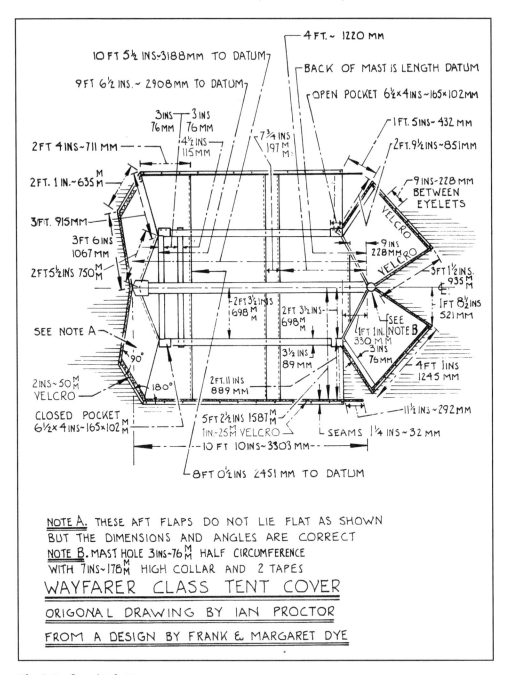

NOTE A. THESE AFT FLAPS DO NOT LIE FLAT AS SHOWN BUT THE DIMENSIONS AND ANGLES ARE CORRECT
NOTE B. MAST HOLE 3INS~76M HALF CIRCUMFERENCE WITH 7INS~178M HIGH COLLAR AND 2 TAPES

WAYFARER CLASS TENT COVER

ORIGONAL DRAWING BY IAN PROCTOR

FROM A DESIGN BY FRANK & MARGARET DYE

The 'Wayfarer' Mk II tent

Notes supplied by Margaret Dye:

To assemble: Push up gooseneck. Set boom on crutches. Tie mast sleeve of tent round mast, having put tent over boom. Skipper and crew work on separate sides. They slide battens into pockets or tent, and clip front battens onto shrouds. Plastic tubing at bottom of shrouds locates battens. Tent is pulled back towards transom, fastening bottom of tent along sides of dinghy.

The openings at stern, bow and shrouds can be sealed or left open according to the weather. The sides can be rolled up, leaving only the roof in position.

CHAPTER 9

Navigation and Pilotage

The basis of navigation in an open boat is no different from that in any other craft. The detail differs – sometimes a great deal. Everything has to be made weatherproof, waterproof and fatigue-proof.

As much work as possible is done before going afloat. All the local tide flows and heights are calculated and marked on a slate or on a piece of paper, ideally the waterproof type sold in yacht chandlers, which is put in a clear plastic pocket. This may be fixed on a locker front and some oilskins have such pockets, nominally for racing instructions. They are on the knee of the oilskin trousers for easy vision.

The characteristics of lights and buoys which figure prominently on the route are written in bold letters on the same paper or full notepad. Or they may be chalked on an area of deck, or buoyancy tank front, which has been painted with that slate-grey compound used to make blackboards. Yet another useful surface for the navigator is a piece of pale coloured Formica glued to the deck or any horizontal surface. Pencil notes can be jotted on this and wiped off after use.

The charts are copiously annotated with the extra information dinghy sailors need, such as landing places, the precise corner of a bay where there is the best mooring ground (as opposed to the general location of the anchor mark in the bay, which is all the hydrographer knows about), the location of fresh water taps and streams and the 'know-how' gained from pilot books and other yachtsmen.

On my charts I use coloured biros to show transits. These are two objects in line and they are among the best friends of the dinghy navigator. For example, a line is drawn through a buoy and a prominent church spire, or through a headland and the north edge of an island. When these two objects are seen in line, they give an exact position on the chart. An intelligent guess is made as to how far off the nearest object of the two seems to be, and then we have a very fair idea of where the boat is. Certainly the transit line is unarguable, only the distance along it may be in doubt. To get the distance off there are two good tricks which help. The first is 'Must be ... Can't be...' which is shorthand for guessing the least possible and the greatest possible distances which an object is from a boat. It works like this:

The helmsman, or the jib sheet hand, or both together, look at a buoy, or lighthouse, or whatever the object is, and decide that –

'It must be at least 2 miles away ...'

'... but it can't be 4 miles away ...'

A Wanderer class dinghy going well in a good breeze. If she was out on a full day's cruise, the crew would not be able to sit out like that from morning to evening and they would have shortened sail.

The assumption is that it is half way between these two limits, so a circle on the chart is sketched about 3 miles off.

This approximating technique can be carried a stage further. If the two people on board each do the first stage in their heads, without saying anything to the other, they each come up with a figure on their own. By working silently neither influences the other. They then say out loud what their guess is. The two guesses are added together and divided by two, thus further increasing the chances of accuracy. If one person is experienced and one a beginner, it may pay to bias the answer towards the more practised guess.

To be any good, this technique needs working up. As the boat sails down a known estuary or along the home stretch of shore, the crew should measure distances on the chart, then look at them over the water. After a time the reverse procedure is tried. Now objects are sighted and their distances guessed, then the estimate checked on the chart. This has to be done in different weather conditions, in the evening, at night, and so on. After spending a few minutes each day, it's amazing how efficiency improves.

Another primitive way of getting a sight line and even a rough position fix, is by using ferries. These ply along fixed lines from the same departure port to the same destination, day after day. They tend to leave and depart on time except during the summer rush period. Even then, certain ferries seem to be good time keepers. Armed with a ferry timetable it is possible to get a useful, but never infallible position fix. The ship's course is marked on the chart and, though she may stray away from it, she is unlikely to be far off, so the only question is, when sighted, how far along the course has she travelled? Knowing the departure and arrival times and measuring the distance along the track gives the ship's speed. If she leaves at say 11.00 a.m., travels 120 miles in six hours and is sighted at 3.00 p.m., then:

$$\text{Ship's speed} = \frac{\text{Distance}}{\text{Time taken}} = \frac{120}{6} = 20 \text{ knots.}$$

Departure is at 11.00 a.m., sighting at 3.00 p.m., so she has been steaming for four hours at 20 knots and has therefore travelled 80 miles. Mark 80 miles off from the departure along the line between the two ports and that is roughly where she is. Of course, if she does not run you down you have to assess how far you are from her approximate position. This sort of primitive navigation technique is a great help because it confirms that dead reckoning and navigation is nothing more than the continuous checking of what we all hope is where we are.

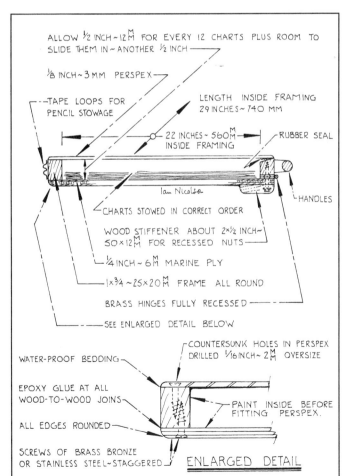

Chart case and table

This case is easily made up and the perspex top can be used for plotting courses by the navigator. The size suits standard folded charts and the edge which opens is sealed with a strip of glued rubber tape which should keep water out. A cabin hook each end will prevent accidental opening.

The wood stiffener which is recessed for the nuts can be fitted with hooks or velcro so that it clips onto a thwart or other structural part of the boat.

Successful navigation consists of painstaking plotting and cross checking as often as the crew can manage. It is combined with a determination never to believe anything until it has been proved three times, and never to panic. If the lighthouse which has been expected does not show up, or the lead line gives a depth which does not tally with the dead reckoning, there can be a great surge of fright. Remember that navigators from time immemorial have been lost. At critical times in history both Noah and Columbus had serious navigational difficulties.

The answer is to gather information, to start from the last known position, and to work out the dead reckoning again. If the navigator is still uncertain, then when in doubt turn offshore since trouble starts when boats meet land – with a bump.

If still lost, sail for something prominent like a big lighthouse. Aim off to one side, then when land is sighted, the way to turn will be known. This 'aiming-off' is standard procedure for experienced small-boat navigators. They never aim directly at their destination, but always set a course to arrive at the landfall upwind of the harbour they wish to reach. When they sight land, they know they are to windward of the haven and they sail close to the coast, as near as is safe, then run downwind (or sometimes downtide if that makes more sense) till they can identify precisely where they are.

A lot of amateurs work with magnetic courses and bearings all the time, though professionals do not. On a chart the inner magnetic rose will be out of date the year after the chart is printed. In practice, these variations are small and in an open boat which is jumping about it is hard to get accuracies of better than 5 degrees. The navigator will struggle to keep his inaccuracies down as much as possible, but they will creep in constantly. This is one reason why all the courses likely to be sailed are drawn on the charts at home before the voyage commences. Not only is each predicted track drawn in and labelled with the magnetic course and distance, but also all the rhum lines to intermediate harbours and places of refuge are drawn. Since this book was first written, cheap handheld GPS instruments have become widely available. Provided spare batteries are on board there are now few navigation worries.

Parallel Rulers and Dividers

Working on the dining-room table it is easy to work the parallel rules. Afloat, these gadgets seize up unless they are slightly sloppy and kept lubricated. This is why so many people use the Davies parallel rule, which is a square of transparent plastic with parallel grid marks all over it and degrees all round the edge.

In the same way, traditional dividers corrode and their sharp points dig right through charts, fingers and oilskins as the boat lurches over the waves. No wonder dinghy sailors like the simple plastic scale rule for measuring distances, especially as it can be laid alongside the Davies protractor to slide it across the chart.

Compasses

The compass on the boat has to be mounted where it can be seen by the helmsman who may be sitting out or he may be down to leeward to keep the boat heeled in light airs. A central compass is often unsatisfactory, especially if the boat has a steel centreboard. A pair of compasses let into port and starboard side decks costs twice as much as one compass, but the advantages are so numerous there are hardly any arguments against this arrangement. If the owner is very hard up, he should consider a single movable compass which can be clipped safely in several different places. Each clip must have a lock to keep the compass in place even during a capsize.

A hand-bearing compass of the type which has a built-in 'beta' light so that it can be used at night, but needs no battery, is a tremendous help. The kind with a rubber shock-absorbing 'tyre' and a length of cord so that it can be worn round the neck and kept in a pocket is hard to beat. It can be used one-handed while steering with the other. If the safe entry line into a harbour is, say, 310 degrees magnetic, the crew sight the entrance regularly. They may first observe it at 260 degrees and a few minutes later at 265 degrees. They relax for a few minutes and then take another sight. The bearing has jumped to 285 degrees and very soon after it is 300 degrees. This is a warning that the tide is whirling the boat past the entrance and it is probably time to turn inshore. Once on the correct bearing, the crew should continue to sight the harbour mouth through the hand-bearer, in case the tide is sweeping the boat out of the safe channel.

The main compasses must be of the type which are unaffected by heeling and should have a card diameter of at least 3 ½ in (90 mm). The grid type has a lot to recommend it because it is virtually impossible to steer the wrong course even when tired, once the grid has been correctly set. Just as important, the grid makes it easy to keep the right course when sitting some distance from the compass, or when well off to one side.

For night sailing, lighting from beneath, with a rheostat to vary the brightness, is needed. However, lots of people dislike the extra complication of wired-in lighting because it is easily ruined by salt water. Instead they just use a hand torch, even though this is more likely to spoil the night vision; also it takes up the remaining hand not being used to hold the tiller. But then we've always known that dinghy sailors must have more hands than an octopus.

The high cost of good compasses, which are big enough to give reliable steering, is offset by their long life. Some owners take their compasses from one boat to the next, though when selling it is essential to tell the buyer that the compasses do not go with the vessel.

Echo Sounders

Considering their complexity, echo sounders are relatively cheap. Admittedly, if they are immersed they are a write-off and they cannot stand even moderate doses of water. They have to be kept encased in transparent plastic bags which must be loose enough to allow the knobs to be turned on through the bag. The smallest size of open

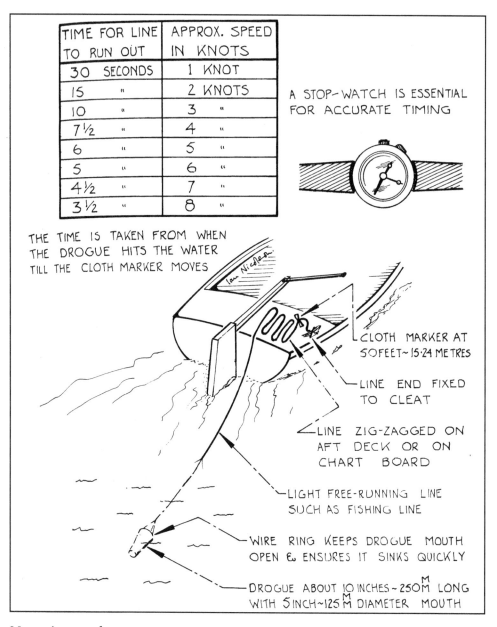

TIME FOR LINE TO RUN OUT	APPROX. SPEED IN KNOTS
30 SECONDS	1 KNOT
15 "	2 KNOTS
10 "	3 "
7½ "	4 "
6 "	5 "
5 "	6 "
4½ "	7 "
3½ "	8 "

A STOP-WATCH IS ESSENTIAL FOR ACCURATE TIMING

THE TIME IS TAKEN FROM WHEN THE DROGUE HITS THE WATER TILL THE CLOTH MARKER MOVES

CLOTH MARKER AT 50 FEET ~ 15·24 METRES

LINE END FIXED TO CLEAT

LINE ZIG-ZAGGED ON AFT DECK OR ON CHART BOARD

LIGHT FREE-RUNNING LINE SUCH AS FISHING LINE

WIRE RING KEEPS DROGUE MOUTH OPEN & ENSURES IT SINKS QUICKLY

DROGUE ABOUT 10 INCHES ~ 250 MM LONG WITH 5 INCH ~ 125 MM DIAMETER MOUTH

Measuring speed

It is easy to make this simple type of log, especially as the drogue can be a child's plastic bucket with reinforced handle and a small weight bolted on to ensure instant but not too rapid sinking. As with all simple gadgets, the first thing to do after making up the equipment is to try it again and again till the crew can use it in all weathers, and all the 'bugs' have been worked out of it.

The line must run out smoothly, and the timing must be accurate. It starts as the drogue starts to pull the line out, and continues till the cloth marker moves. Do not wait till the marker, which is just a piece of brightly coloured cloth tied to the line at the 50 ft mark, slides overboard.

It is important that the line runs out smoothly, so it is not coiled, and must not be laid on an aft thwart, nor must it catch or drop on the transom top. Practice and checking over known distances and times ensure accuracy.

boat likely to have an echo sounder is about 16 ft (5.5 m). It is, as always, a question of how much room there is on the boat and how much cash the crew can scrape together.

Echo sounders give continuous soundings, they save the crew a lot of labour, they work in water too deep for easy sounding with a lead and they are extremely accurate most of the time. Of all the electronic gadgets found in small boats, they have the highest standard of reliability and are the most popular.

There are versions which have alarms. These can be set to warn the crew that they are getting into shallow water. They can also tell the helmsman he is moving offshore and getting into deep water when he wants to stay over a shallow patch, perhaps to avoid steamers in a fog, or he may wish to work his way along a shoreline at night.

On balance, an echo sounder is well down the list of extras most people will fit, simply because there is so large a chance that it will be ruined by water getting in, even though the plastic bag encasing it has three tight elastic bands at the point where the electric cable goes through to the transducer in the bottom of the boat.

Lead and Line

A simple lead and line is just the opposite. It is cheap to make and as the ideal type is not sold, there is no choice but to make it up. It never wears out yet it stands up to unlimited immersion and abuse. The lead must be a little over 2 lb (1 kilo) for use when the boat is sailing fast. This works out at a cylinder roughly 6 in long and 1 in diameter (150 mm × 25 mm).

To fabricate a lead, drill a 1 in (25 mm) diameter hole 7 in (175 mm) long in a block of well dried wood at least 4 in × 4 in (100 mm × 100 mm) in section. Pour molten lead carefully into the hole, wearing protective clothing and goggles to avoid being splashed by hot metal. Split the wood open, and with saw and file shape the bottom to a half sphere, then taper the top, as shown in the sketch. If after trials the lead is found to be too heavy, it can be shortened or a light version, also shown in the sketch, can be made.

It is traditional and easiest to use a lead from the leeside, but this is no good if the crew have to sit to windward to hold the boat upright, so it is best to practise from both sides. The line is coiled to a diameter of about a foot (300 mm) and the lead swung forward with the outboard hand. It must be heaved so far ahead of the boat that when it touches the sea bed the line is vertical and the depth is read off on the thin rope. The marks on the line are designed so that they can be felt and the depth known even in the dark.

At first it is hard to keep a lead going for 10 minutes, but this is just another skill that comes with practice. I'll never forget the excitement and satisfaction of sounding with a lead across the sandbanks of the Thames Estuary in fog for one and a half hours and picking up the hoped-for buoy at the end of that time.

When sounding in extra deep water it may be necessary to stop the boat, or slow right down, and possibly add rope on the end of the line for sufficient depth. It will soon be found by practice just how far the weight has to be swung forward (just

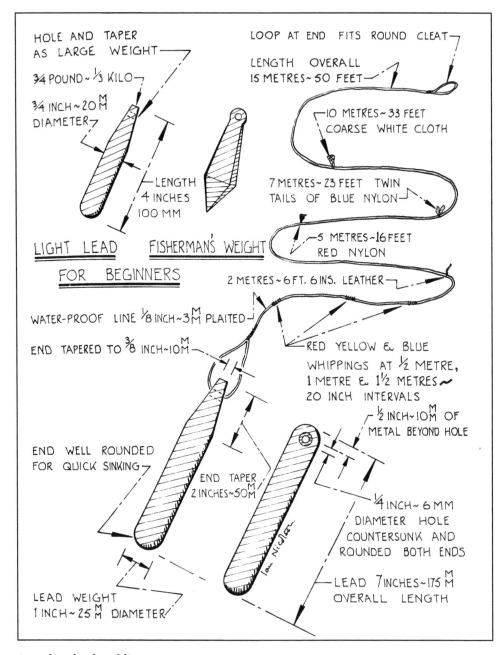

Sounding lead and line

The line should be well stretched before being marked. It is best to use the line for a couple of weekends before putting the marks on it. These marks should be sewn on, and they are designed for use at night as the material can be felt to identify it in the dark.

The lead shown at the bottom is a general purpose one, too light for deep-sea work, but fine for most coastal conditions. The one shown top left is only suitable for shallow waters, and if it cannot be made, the fisherman's weight can be bought in angling shops.

The line should be waterproof and plaited, and is best kept on a wood board so that it dries out quickly and does not tangle when stowed.

above sea level) to ensure the line comes vertical when the boat sails up to where the lead is touching the bottom.

The base of the lead is rounded to encourage the weight to sink fast. In the old days it was usual to have a ½ in (12 mm) deep recess roughly gouged out of the bottom of the lead and this was filled with tallow. As the weight touched the seabed, sand or shingle or shells stuck to the tallow, so when the lead was hauled back the crew could compare the sample with the notes on the chart.

This method is satisfying when it works, but there is a good deal against it. Few people want to carry a tin of tallow, though some of the softer soaps will do instead, and there are stories of using butter and margarine. When the seabed is muddy the water may wash the sample off as the lead is hauled in. This is a nuisance and applying the sticky substance in rough conditions can be messy. It is necessary to take more than one sample, especially near those harbours where there is a dredger regularly depositing soil at the estuary mouth. In Nelson's day some of these techniques were easier.

CHAPTER 10

Food, Drink and Cookers

A friend bought an old Dragon class boat and asked me to crew in his first race. It was a typical Clyde summer day, blowing gustily, with driving rain each time a black cloud went over. Even going out to the starting line we were swept by green water running deep along the deck.

We pumped before the start and we pumped when we had a brief moment on each run. Even so there often seemed to be half the ocean in the bilge and the other half pouring aft along the deck. On the second beat my attention was taken away from the genoa briefly by the slurp and gurgle of the water which sploshed back and forward over the floorboards. I looked into the cuddy and there was my lunch box floating. Twice I rescued it, but what with the motion and the way the water kept getting deeper in the boat during the more hectic periods, the box launched itself twice more.

When the race was over and we were celebrating a surprising third place with all sorts of famous fast boats nicely astern, I opened the plastic box ... and all the food inside was dry. But not too dry. When afloat, conditions are often unpleasant and food must offset this by being fresh, tasty, interesting and varied. It must also be seaworthy.

When buying food for even a short voyage, it is important to choose things which are easy to stow and hard to spoil. In the Second World War rice was packed into sacks, then a second much larger sack put over the inner one and carefully sewn up. These double sacks of rice were thrown out of aeroplanes without parachutes (admittedly from no great height) to waiting troops below. When the food hit the ground the inner sacks burst, but no rice was lost as it was all contained by the outer sack. Rice is great on boats too, like other farinaceous materials, because it can stand up to rough treatment. Oatmeal, macaroni and spaghetti, as well as dried vegetables, can be packed into plastic bags and if the anchor is accidentally dumped on top, no damage will ensue. The same cannot be said for cream cakes or grapes.

The best fresh vegetables to take are those which are boat-worthy by nature. Potatoes, carrots and turnips can be wetted by salt water (but not for too long) and still be used. Leeks and cabbages will stand up to a moderate amount of rough and tumble and the heavy tread of sea-booted feet. In contrast, lettuce and tomatoes are pleasant to eat, especially in summer conditions, but they have to be protected by stout plastic or metal boxes and both go bad rather too easily.

Tinned food is heavy but it can stand up to conditions afloat. Labels have to be soaked off and the contents named with an indelible marker or paint.

Dried food in packets needs additional packing, as the sachets on their own will not stand up to sliding about inside a half-empty locker.

In fact, most foods need wrapping in at least one plastic bag, and often an inner and outer one, for protection and to keep out water and dirt. If water is in short supply, the packets of dried food are opened well in advance so that the damp atmosphere is soaked up. It's amazing how much this food swells and blots up moisture when the packet is opened and shaken up every so often so that the contents are turned over. This saves fresh water.

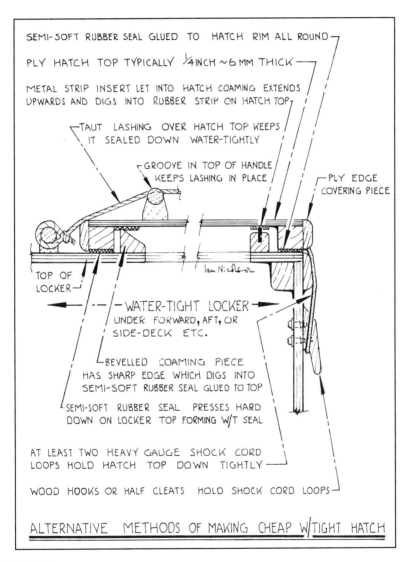

SEMI-SOFT RUBBER SEAL GLUED TO HATCH RIM ALL ROUND

PLY HATCH TOP TYPICALLY ¼ INCH ~6 MM THICK

METAL STRIP INSERT LET INTO HATCH COAMING EXTENDS UPWARDS AND DIGS INTO RUBBER STRIP ON HATCH TOP

TAUT LASHING OVER HATCH TOP KEEPS IT SEALED DOWN WATER-TIGHTLY

GROOVE IN TOP OF HANDLE KEEPS LASHING IN PLACE

PLY EDGE COVERING PIECE

TOP OF LOCKER

Ian Nicholson

← — WATER-TIGHT LOCKER →
UNDER FORWARD, AFT, OR SIDE-DECK ETC.

BEVELLED COAMING PIECE HAS SHARP EDGE WHICH DIGS INTO SEMI-SOFT RUBBER SEAL GLUED TO TOP

SEMI-SOFT RUBBER SEAL PRESSES HARD DOWN ON LOCKER TOP FORMING W/T SEAL

AT LEAST TWO HEAVY GAUGE SHOCK CORD LOOPS HOLD HATCH TOP DOWN TIGHTLY

WOOD HOOKS OR HALF CLEATS HOLD SHOCK CORD LOOPS

ALTERNATIVE METHODS OF MAKING CHEAP W/TIGHT HATCH

Watertight lockers

The most important alteration needed, when changing a boat from racing to cruising, or adapting a boat for cruising, is the provision of dry stowage. Sealed areas under the forward and aft decks may be used, or the insides of the side buoyancy tanks. Each compartment must have a good-sized access hatch, and this sketch shows ways of making these inexpensively.

Both techniques use inner and outer watertight seals and cheap closure arrangements with no metal fittings. If the hatch tops are bigger than about 12 in (300 mm) they will need glued-on stiffeners.

Best of all, put the food into a wide plastic box and stir it round regularly. To save fresh water further most savoury foods can be reconstituted with a mixture of one part salt water to five parts fresh.

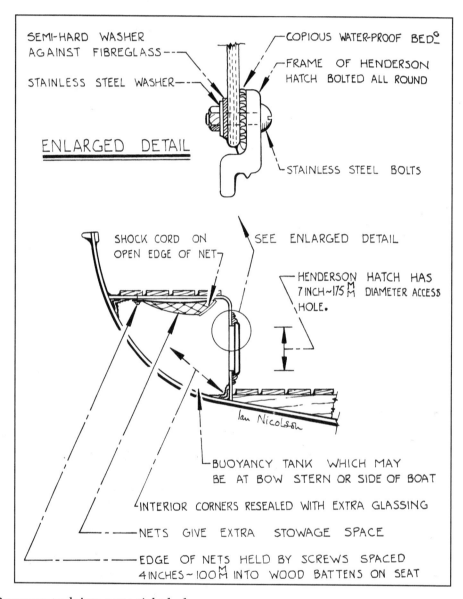

SEMI-HARD WASHER AGAINST FIBREGLASS

STAINLESS STEEL WASHER

COPIOUS WATER-PROOF BED^G

FRAME OF HENDERSON HATCH BOLTED ALL ROUND

ENLARGED DETAIL

STAINLESS STEEL BOLTS

SHOCK CORD ON OPEN EDGE OF NET

SEE ENLARGED DETAIL

HENDERSON HATCH HAS 7 INCH ~ 175 M DIAMETER ACCESS HOLE.

Ian Nicolson

BUOYANCY TANK WHICH MAY BE AT BOW STERN OR SIDE OF BOAT

INTERIOR CORNERS RESEALED WITH EXTRA GLASSING

NETS GIVE EXTRA STOWAGE SPACE

EDGE OF NETS HELD BY SCREWS SPACED 4 INCHES ~ 100 M INTO WOOD BATTENS ON SEAT

Buoyancy tank into watertight locker

Whatever material is used for the hull construction, if there are built-in buoyancy tanks they can be converted to valuable watertight lockers. The insides may need resealing, and if there is any doubt about the watertight integrity, this work should be done.

Henderson hatches are usually the best access doors to fit because they are well-developed, reliable, long-lasting and strong, besides being easy to fit. Their main limitation is the small size of the access hole they have.

Part of the pre-cruising work should include planning meals for each day. It is best to have six successive days of ordinary meals with a specially luxurious one on the seventh day, to have something special to look forward to, and to vary the diet. The daily enthusiasm of the crew may be dominated by the wind speed and direction, but the quality and variations in the diet are almost as critical.

When the food is being made ready before going afloat, it is no bad thing to put each day's supplies into a separate, watertight bag, with vulnerable items each in its own bag. Then if there is a capsize, much of the food will remain edible. For an offshore trip it might be better to have each meal in a polythene bag or box. Experienced crews grade the meals according to how easy they are to cook afloat. Then if the weather is fine, they select a relatively elaborate meal, leaving the super-simple ones for wild, wet days.

Drink

Alcohol is a mixed blessing on board. It is sensible not to imbibe any until the anchor is down and the boat made snug for the night. But what happens if the wind gets up from an awkward quarter and the boat has to be moved? Or if some idiot helmsman comes hurtling into the anchorage out of control and needs rescuing ... or dodging ... or hauling off the mud? The best rule seems to be: one tot per person per evening, or one pint of beer (or its equivalent) works well; more is taking a risk; successful cruising involves no risks.

In wet or cold weather hot fluids are particularly good because they are easy to consume and give water and nutrition at the same time. Soup, cocoa, in fact most hot drinks restore morale and provide energy. Some people store cocoa powder, dried milk and sugar mixed together in the correct proportions, then they only have to add hot water.

Fresh milk is handy because it can be used hot or cold, it makes dull dishes interesting and it goes into so many menus. It is best stowed in a plastic container with a screw top about 1 ½ in (40 mm) diameter. This sort of top makes pouring easy, but it is not so small as to prevent efficient cleaning and scalding of the container.

Those large thermos flasks which have wide lids and taps at the bottom are now popular in spite of their price. Before getting under way in the morning they are filled with a favourite hot drink, so this beverage is literally 'on tap' all day. These thermoses must be well fixed down – more break than wear out. If buying an ordinary thermos without a tap go for the unbreakable stainless steel type. The extra cost is worthwhile. It is usual to have a moderate or large breakfast, including a hot drink, then to eat snacks during the day, and to have a substantial hot evening meal. Of course, this is no good to teenagers who want copious, solid food at frequent intervals with plenty of bulky edibles to fill the gaps in the moments between meals. Maybe if they were given a massive plate of porridge in the morning instead of that chopped-up cardboard called 'cereals' they would not suffer the pangs of hunger so often. Perhaps it's my Scottish bias, but I think that before setting out to brave the seas, a vast plate of porridge is unbeatable. It's even comfortable as a basis for seasickness! Oatmeal is great in all sorts of dishes from thickening soups to coating on any fish you have caught, before frying.

Oatmeal Flapjack

Far better than bought biscuits or cake is flapjack, another miracle made with oatmeal. It is made like this: Melt in a medium-sized saucepan 10 oz (275 g) of block margarine, then add 6 oz (165 g) of demerara sugar and 2 tablespoons of golden syrup. Stir in a pound (450 g) of porridge oats, not oatmeal. When the sticky mess is well stirred, spoon it into two 7 in (175 mm) diameter sandwich tins which have been well greased. The mixture must be pressed down into the tins. It is baked for about 30 minutes in an oven at around 350–375 degrees F (Gas Mark 4). I like the resulting biscuits softish so I take flapjack out of the oven before the top has browned, whereas my wife likes it crisp, so she cooks it a little longer until the edges are clearly darkening. As soon as the tins are out of the oven a knife is drawn across them, then at right angles five times. This makes twelve thick fingers. Leave the flapjack in the tins until it is cold and hard. I like to make sure mine is OK so I eat some while it is still hot. Fabulous!

Flapjack is, of course, made at home before the voyage begins. Food preparation at home is important because, even when in a sheltered mooring, it is hard to do any serious cooking. Heating up food is about the limit for most people, though there are hardy souls who turn out gastronomic triumphs on single burner cookers. Even they tend to do as much work in the convenience of the home kitchen before going afloat.

Guide to Quantity

As a rough guide, most people need about 2 ½ lb (1.13 kg) of food per day, though some people can get through much more, especially in cold weather when working hard ... and dinghy cruising can be energetic work. An average man needs roughly 3,000 calories per day when working physically. In extreme conditions, when cold or wet and when getting a great deal of exercise, a fit, tough, tall man may need as much as 6,500 calories.

At the other end of the scale, if a boat is far from supplies and the food stocks are running low, a pound (about ½ kilo) of food will keep an active person going well enough. People can last for days on only 850 calories. In fact, shortage of water is far more serious than lack of food. So for a long voyage, make sure the reserves are biased towards spare water rather than extra food.

The standard allowance of water is half a gallon (2.2 litres) per person per day, but this is generous and plenty of people have lived for a long time on 2 pints (about a litre) of water per day. I've been happy using only one pint (½ litre) per day for days on end during an ocean cruise, when getting extra moisture from tinned food. Naturally, these quantities include no allowance for washing. It is in hot weather that the half gallon per person per day ration is needed. Shortage of fluids in sweltering sunny conditions soon becomes dangerous, whereas it takes days for a lack of food to make a serious difference to a person's well-being. Of course, everyone soon feels hungry when meals do not arrive on time, but even that feeling becomes blunted after a time.

Cookers

The simplest way to cook is to make a campfire on the shore. This is cheap, and provided there is plenty of fuel, there is no difficulty getting ample heat. It may be necessary to carry some fuel, or at least kindling on the boat, and perhaps a simple wind shelter, also two forked sticks and a crossbar, for suspending a cooking pan over the flames. Camping shops can provide the necessary gear. It's a sad fact that along many coastlines fires are not permitted, or the shore is unsuitable for beaching the boat. On the whole, it is almost always best cooking in the boat.

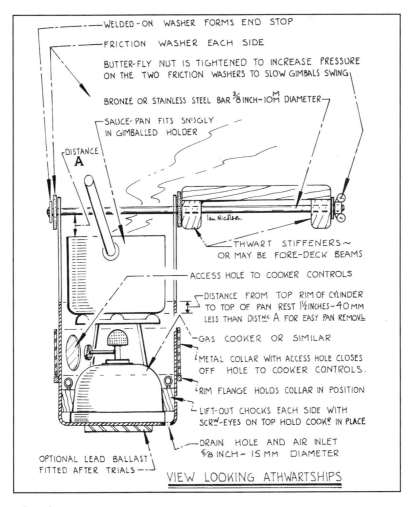

Spill-proof cooker
This easily-made cooker consists of a gas or liquid fuel camping stove housed in a metal cylinder. The bottom of the cylinder has a blanking off plate, complete with drain hole and air inlet. Thin strips of metal extend up from the top rim of the cylinder. At the top of these strips there are holes which slide onto the horizontal bar. By tightening the butterfly nut, the rate at which the cooker swings is damped, as the friction washers come into play.

Most people use a simple bottled gas cooker sold in chandlers and camping shops. The gas bottles may be of the disposable type, or the larger refillable type. The former are expensive if the boat is used a lot. Both types can also be used with lanterns, so one lot of gas can be used for two purposes.

For a long journey, when a lot of fuel has to be carried, it is usual to have one of the traditional 'primus' types of stoves. These burn paraffin (kerosene) and they have

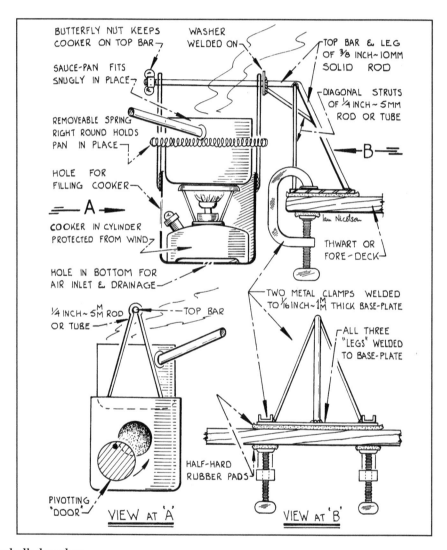

Gimballed cooker

This design of gimbals is ideal when the thwart is low, and there is no room to swing a cooker beneath it. The cooker itself is housed in a cylinder with a closed base, to protect the flame from strong winds. The 'gantry' which supports the gimballed cooker is quickly taken off the swinging unit, and it only takes a second to unscrew the two clamps, then the cooker, in two parts, is ready for stowing. The clamps cannot damage the boat's seat or foredeck thanks to the padding on the clamp paws.

been made reliable by generations of improvement and use in tough conditions. They need methylated spirits to start them, which is a nuisance, but they are economical.

Frank and Margaret Dye, perhaps the most experienced dinghy cruisers there have been, favoured the 'Optimus' petrol (gasolene) cooker because they have carried out tests in strong winds. They found that cookers without a strong flame could under bad conditions splutter away without ever throwing out enough heat to boil a kettle. This confirms the need to have a proper sheltered location for the cooker, usually under a thwart. Just as important, there must be gimbals so that the cooker stays upright. Fiddles are also needed and these should be the type which clutch the pan firmly. Some people have a kettle, but I prefer a prospector's coffee pot. It can be used to make porridge, eggs can be boiled in it, using salt water which is then used for washing up, and for tea one just boils the water, then throws in the tea, leaving the pot to bubble away; this gives a wonderfully strong brew. The stove fiddles should be adjustable, or include clamps, to hold the coffee pot in place.

It may be argued that the crew will only cook in sheltered harbours, or when the boat is aground, so they do not need gimbals. However, the owners of high-powered motorboats are just waiting round the corner to zap past at full throttle throwing off a wash which capsizes the dinner all over the floorboards.

For emergencies, such as very bad weather, there are self-heating tins. These are self-contained and need no cooker. They last for eighteen months and can stand up to rough conditions afloat. They are not cheap, but when the crew are cold and miserable, they are wonderful morale-restorers.

CHAPTER 11

Safety Equipment

Like everything else which is bought for cruising in open boats, the safety gear should be the best available, meticulously maintained, and renewed whenever there is doubt about its effectiveness. Of course, this is an expensive attitude, but safety is only achieved by taking a technician's approach, not an accountant's.

For people who are hard up, Christmas and birthdays are opportunities for getting new or better safety gear. My family would never think of giving me a yacht club tie when they know that my bilge pump needs a set of spares, or one of my waterproof torches is beginning to corrode inside.

Just what constitutes the best choice for each item is something which provokes arguments. This is partly because different types of cruising need slightly different gear. Also, experience using safety gear tends to be dramatic and this leaves sharp memories. Anyone who has tried to get a distress rocket to soar vertically upwards in a very strong wind and seen it fly horizontally as soon as it is launched, so that it never achieves a sensible altitude, is likely to be against rockets forever. This is unfair because powerful rockets will struggle upwards even in ferocious winds, but this type is so heavy, bulky and expensive that it is not practical to carry them in most small boats.

The following comments are therefore based on various experiences. After a year or two of cruising in open boats some people will have their own ideas which may result in a few changes. Besides, every year there are improvements which outdate existing equipment.

Life Jackets and Buoyancy Aids

It is obvious that there must be a life jacket on board for each person. The only trouble is that when wearing one it is hard to be active because movement above the waist is so restricted. As a result a standard Government approved life jacket can cause accidents, especially if the crew are tired. There are more problems: the crew may be sailing downwind in breezy but hot weather, so they may have no oilskins on, though they will be wearing life jackets, very rightly as it is the correct thing to do whenever the wind pipes up. What happens when the time comes to put on oilskin jackets? There is the struggle to get out of the life jackets, into the oilies, then back into the preservers. This is just the sort of hassle which causes long moments of inattention and a capsize.

After a lot of hesitation I have come to the conclusion that for most, but not all, open boat cruising under sail, an approved buoyancy aid is often safer than a life jacket. Of course, this is one of those choices which must be wrong at times. Anyone floating free from the dinghy for a long time is safer in a life jacket, but it is a cardinal rule that no one leaves a capsized boat, even if land or help seems quite close. The boat is big and buoyant and will support her crew well, besides showing up far better than one or two people in the water.

Buoyancy aids are like thin undernourished life jackets. They support a person in the water but do not keep the head upright or turn an unconscious person the right way up, nor do they keep the wearer high in the water. Against this, they can be worn all day without discomfort and without noticeably hampering activity. They may well keep the wearer warmer than if he were in a life jacket, especially as they can be worn under oilskins.

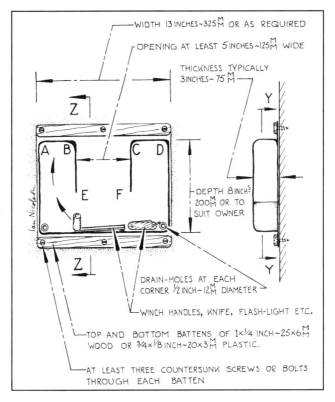

Capsize-proof stowage bags

This type of stowage bag is ideal for items of gear which cannot conveniently be tied to the boat, but are wanted often. If the boat turns over, the gear tumbles into the recesses at A-B or C-D instead of going overboard.

These bags will have to be specially made up by a sailmaker and will be of Terylene (Dacron), PVC or man-made canvas or something similar. The entrance to the bag, at E-F, must be wide enough to get the gear in, and owners should ideally make a mock-up before selecting the dimensions which suit them. These bags must not be stuffed full, in fact the gear must be loose inside, and the points E and F must be about half way down the bag. The left view is at Y-Y and the right view at Z-Z.

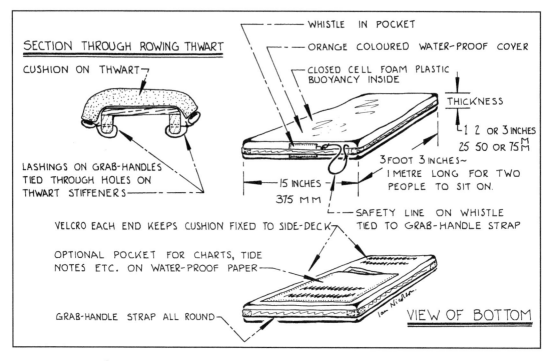

Buoyant cushions

The cushion shown here will have about 15 lbs (7 kg) of buoyancy for every 1 in (25 mm) of thickness. It may be used when sailing, laid along the side deck, or on the rowing thwart when using the oars. Some people will prefer smaller cushions, one for each member of the crew. In an emergency these cushions can be used as fenders, or to protect the hull from rough ground.

Buoyancy aids seldom have lights or whistles attached as some life jackets do. However a light and whistle is best on the oilskins, properly attached at all times.

There is one type of life jacket which seems to be the best of all worlds. It has a certain amount of built-in buoyancy in the form of closed-cell foam, so it is, in effect, like a buoyancy aid. However, there is also an inflatable bladder inside the outer covering which can be blown up by a CO_2 cylinder or by a mouth tube. It sounds just perfect, so it is important to appreciate the snags; if the CO_2 cylinder is activated when the jacket is worn under an oilskin, there will not be enough room for the bladder to expand and it may burst. Just as serious, this type of jacket has a relatively short life and needs annual maintenance by the manufacturer. If it is to inflate automatically when an unconscious man falls in the water it must have an expensive self-activating valve. More money and more gadgetry!

I have used inflatable jackets on several occasions and this once provoked the remark: 'We can always tell how dangerous you think things are getting by the amount you blow up your life jacket'.

This type of jacket does not keep the wearer warm as effectively as most buoyancy aids and it does need annual maintenance by the makers. However, it gives as much, or almost as much, flotation when fully inflated, as a Government approved type and it can be worn partly full all day. It can also be worn under or outside an oilskin, but for full inflation it must be outside the oilskin.

Personal Lifeline or Safely Harness

Anyone who has done a lot of dinghy racing will hesitate to wear a lifeline when cruising because there are always too many ropes swirling around inside a dinghy. However, long-distance sailing is very different from an afternoon's race. The risk of being separated from the boat in the event of a capsize is much more serious and, as the boat is kept more under control, with less sail up, the extra complication is acceptable.

Standard harnesses are made of webbing or tape and the joining line may also be of tape. The straps are fitted high up round the body so that there is no risk that the head will be pulled under or the breath be driven out of the body. A harness is far safer and more comfortable than the traditional arrangement of a rope knotted round the waist. (A slip knot doubles the danger.)

Harnesses have snap hooks or carbine hooks on their ends and these are engaged onto U-bolts or some similar strong point. As open boats seldom have such fittings, either they

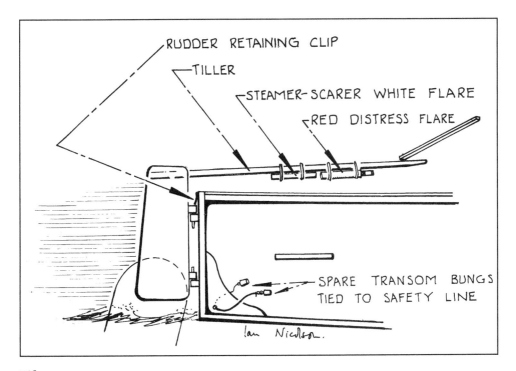

Lifesavers
As navigation lights on an open boat are seldom powerful, some device is needed to warn off big ships and fishing boats. White flares are specially made for this, and they work just like the ordinary distress flares, which of course burn with a startling red glow, or shoot off red stars. It is an excellent idea to have one of each of these flares right to hand, held to the tiller with shock-cord loops.

must be added, or the end of the line is looped round a thwart and clipped back on itself. Whichever way the harness is secured to the boat, it must be clear of all other ropes, so it may pay to fix U-bolts to the boat after a trial sail to determine the best location.

If the harnesses are fixed around thwarts, or onto U-bolts on any part of the hull, the underlying strength of the structure must be double checked. Thwarts are sometimes held by no more than a couple of light bolts or screws each end, on the basis that all the loading is normally downwards, so the fastenings have little work to do. But the sudden jolt of a lifeline pulling aft or athwartships may be much more than the original fastening can stand, so new ones or extra ones will be needed.

First Aid Kit

The usual kit, sold by yacht chandlers, is fine provided that it has been designed by someone who knows about sailing. Most kits have inadequate scissors, so some people throw them away and use the galley scissors instead. Also the instruction book is usually thin and therefore likely to cover all crises except the one in hand. A more comprehensive book makes sense and is handy for light reading when gale-bound.

The adhesive plasters are almost always too few, too small and they need renewing annually. Sun-protecting lotion is not always included and I like to have one of those white lipsticks much used on the ski slopes. Some people will add a medicine to treat diarrhoea and a clinical thermometer. Pills to treat dubious water and disinfectant are not always included in standard packs.

Distress Signals

The number and type of items carried for summoning help varies according to how far offshore the boat is going. In theory all boats, regardless of size, need the same set of signals, because what matters is the distance from the boat in trouble to the potential rescuers, and the thickness of the weather. So any boat going far offshore should carry the same flares and day signals as a big cruising yacht. What happens in practice is that most people go to a chandler and buy something called an 'Inshore Pack' or a 'Coastal Pack'. If the owner really feels that such inadequate sets of lifesaving equipment is all he needs, he should stick to golf or snooker.

Read the descriptions of boats in distress as told by the survivors and the rescuers, and it is clear that shortage of signals is a recurring theme. So for sailing in truly sheltered waters, the minimum to carry is two 'Inshore Packs', and for out-of-harbour voyaging, have at least two 'Coastal Packs'.

In each case one pack should be stowed in its own polythene box and tucked away securely somewhere handy, where it can be reached when the boat is flooded and maybe lying on her side. The other pack should be opened and each distress signal wrapped in its own plastic bag, then secured somewhere very accessible, like under a thwart, held by spring clips or shock cord. In the panic of an emergency one wants to be able to get a flare off quickly in spite of driving spray, cold fingers and a deluge of plain fright. Wise men and women practice letting off flares every Guy Fawkes night in Britain and on the appropriate national holidays in other countries. Warn the neighbours first before the firework display. Last time I practised I set my neighbour's garden on fire. It was getting overgrown anyway, so I don't know why he was so annoyed.

Radar Reflector

The most efficient type of radar reflector is enclosed in a casing which protects the metal plates from damage. These plates are set precisely at right-angles to ensure the incoming radio waves are accurately reflected back to the radar set which sent them. Even quite tiny distortions of the metal plates reduce the effectiveness of the radar reflector, which is why the old-fashioned reflectors are less and less satisfactory, the older and more battered they get.

So much for theory. In practice, an encased radar reflector must be bulky by small boat standards and, because they have to be built to high standards to be any good, they are costly. For anyone going offshore, or sailing in crowded waters in a boat of 16 ft (5 m) or more, it is necessary to put up with the inconvenient bulk and cost. The reflector can be stowed well out of the way until the weather requires its use, and it does not have to be in one of the watertight lockers.

So far as the cost is concerned, at least it needs no maintenance. Like all safety gear, its purchase price seems a waste of money until it is needed. During the time a piece of safety gear is in use the crew (quietly or vociferously sweating with fright) will vow they will never again give a moment's thought to costs when buying safety gear. The cost of all the emergency gear a cruising dinghy can carry is far less than the cost of a bashed-in hull or a funeral.

The higher a reflector is carried, the better it works. It should be secured so that it is held rigidly – so far as possible.

Fire Extinguisher

If the crew cook in a tent there must be at least a small fire extinguisher handy. It is no good saying that a bucket of water can be pitched over a cooker which has got out of control, because inside a boat-tent there is seldom a chance to get the water properly applied quickly.

The type of extinguisher to buy has to be capable of dealing with a burning gas or primus cooker; it has to withstand weathering and the damp, being trodden on and stuffed in a kit bag with other gear. It seldom pays to buy the cheapest. Even a moderate burn on the hand ruins the best cruise, so the extinguisher should be put close, but not right beside the cooker or pressure lantern, before lighting up.

The best type of extinguisher has a control so that it can be turned off before all the contents are expended. A fire-blanket is often more effective than an extinguisher.

Signalling Cloth

This is nothing more than a bright orange Day-Glo waterproof sheet with a large international distress sign, namely a big V on it. It can be quite small, but the bigger it

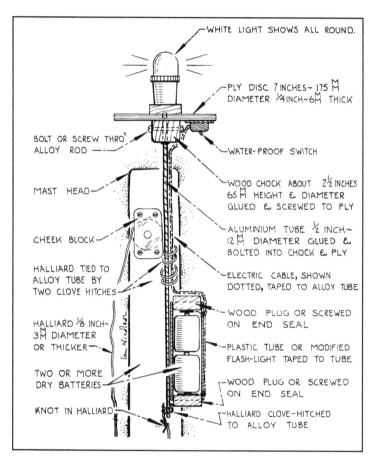

Navigation light

The correct light for a small open boat to display is a white light shining all round and visible from two miles away. The one shown here is made so that it can be hoisted on a flag halliard and, as it has a disc beneath, it will not affect the crew's night vision.

If an aluminium tube is not available a length of bamboo can be used. The access to the batteries must be easy because they will need changing each evening, or even more frequently if the night sail is a long one.

This light can also be used as a 'cabin lantern' when moored up, as it can be hung from the rigging or on the mast, or held by a pair of spring clips round the plastic tube or flashlight body which holds the batteries.

is, the further away it will be seen, so it is usually about 6 ft × 6 ft (2 m) square. It can be used as part of the tent, or even be designed as a storm sail. On some boats it is sewn up into a waterproof bag for stowing gear. There must be strong eyelets on it all round.

After dismasting it is secured to the stump of the spar, or tied to an oar and erected to attract attention. It can be waved like a flag to call for assistance and is much more effective than waving a life jacket. In real trouble it is usual to let off flares, but when these have run out, the signalling cloth comes into play. Also there are some 'intermediate' crises which are not sufficiently serious to warrant the use of a flare, and then the cloth is ideal.

Fog Horn

This is another of those items of safety equipment which a lot of people cruising in a 12 footer (4 m) do not carry. They get away with it because they do not go out in thick weather or if caught out, they dodge so far inshore that no other craft can navigate near them. It all works out well in practice – nearly all the time. Every so often things go wrong. On a short passage between harbours a heavy rain squall blots out visibility, the wind goes, and the boat cannot manoeuvre out of the way of oncoming danger.

It is argued that even if she had a foghorn, it is unlikely to be heard above that outrageous roar which modern diesels make. There is a lot of truth in this and, as the helmsman of a fishing boat is often inside a wheelhouse with the engine close by, he hears very little except his own machinery clatter.

On the other hand, if the boat is run down, and it is shown that there was no foghorn on board, the crew might not get compensation, or it might be much reduced. Besides, not all danger comes in the form of deafened fishermen. A big yacht under sail can smash over a dinghy just as effectively, and the crew of the yacht should be able to hear even a small fog horn in time to sail clear of it.

Certainly, anyone cruising in a 16 ft (5 m) open boat should have a foghorn. The type of brass horn which is blown like a child's trumpet is not loud, but it needs little maintenance and it goes on working as long as the crew have enough puff. It costs about twice as much as the pressurised canister type, but the latter needs a new canister after a very few hours use and each canister costs half the original price. For a serious cruise at least one spare canister has to be carried.

Buckets and Bailers

The oldest joke afloat asks, 'What's the best bilge pump?' and the answer is, 'A frightened yachtsman with a big bucket!' There is no doubt that a bucket has most of the advantages we seek when we want to get water out of a boat. It is cheap and tough, it needs no maintenance and it has few moving parts. It does not clog or block, so it deals with anything floating in the bilge like drowned newspapers, matches and soggy socks.

The best kind of bucket is the thick, rigid rubber type sold in those ironmongers who cater for farmers. A few enlightened chandlers stock them. This type of bucket is strong enough to double as a toilet too.

For ordinary bailing problems the plastic scoop type has lots of virtues. It's compact, shifts a lot of water if used with a swift continuous series of swoops, is unlikely to break, it floats, and has a sensible handle which will take the safety line. Its main trouble (and this applies to all bailers) is that it needs good access to the bottom of the boat. This means that there must be a space where there are no floorboards and no gear stowed and that space must be near the low point inside the hull.

It is quite usual to carry two of these scoops, one near the helmsman and one handy for the jib-sheet hand. They are cheap enough and are available from most chandlers. For anyone who has no access to a chandler, or who likes to make all his own gear, a scoop bailer is easily made from wood, as the Scandinavians do, or out of a plastic bottle or plastic jerrycan. The end is cut off and a handle made of wood screwed on.

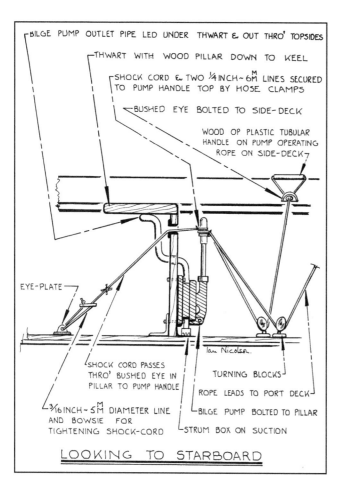

BILGE PUMP OUTLET PIPE LED UNDER THWART & OUT THRO' TOPSIDES

THWART WITH WOOD PILLAR DOWN TO KEEL

SHOCK CORD & TWO ¼ INCH~6M LINES SECURED TO PUMP HANDLE TOP BY HOSE CLAMPS

BUSHED EYE BOLTED TO SIDE-DECK

WOOD OP PLASTIC TUBULAR HANDLE ON PUMP OPERATING ROPE ON SIDE-DECK

EYE-PLATE

Ian Nicolson.

SHOCK CORD PASSES THRO' BUSHED EYE IN PILLAR TO PUMP HANDLE

TURNING BLOCKS

ROPE LEADS TO PORT DECK

³⁄₁₆ INCH~5M DIAMETER LINE AND BOWSIE FOR TIGHTENING SHOCK-CORD

BILGE PUMP BOLTED TO PILLAR

STRUM BOX ON SUCTION

LOOKING TO STARBOARD

Bilge pump operated from side deck

This bilge pump can be operated by the crew from either side deck, so that they can continue to sit well outboard and get rid of bilge water.

The pump is a standard diaphragm type bolted to a specially fitted pillar between the underside of a thwart and the keel. The suction is short and goes into a strum box; the discharge is by pipe and skin fitting through the topsides. In practice, the ropes from the handle would probably extend more aft and not so steeply down towards the blocks on the keel. Also, for continuous use it might be better to have a sheave instead of the bushed fairlead in the pillar.

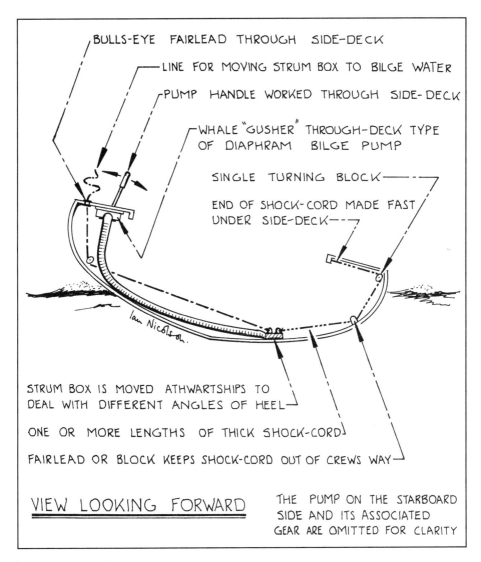

BULLS-EYE FAIRLEAD THROUGH SIDE-DECK

LINE FOR MOVING STRUM BOX TO BILGE WATER

PUMP HANDLE WORKED THROUGH SIDE-DECK

WHALE "GUSHER" THROUGH-DECK TYPE OF DIAPHRAM BILGE PUMP

SINGLE TURNING BLOCK

END OF SHOCK-CORD MADE FAST UNDER SIDE-DECK

Ian Nicolson.

STRUM BOX IS MOVED ATHWARTSHIPS TO DEAL WITH DIFFERENT ANGLES OF HEEL

ONE OR MORE LENGTHS OF THICK SHOCK-CORD

FAIRLEAD OR BLOCK KEEPS SHOCK-CORD OUT OF CREWS WAY

VIEW LOOKING FORWARD

THE PUMP ON THE STARBOARD SIDE AND ITS ASSOCIATED GEAR ARE OMITTED FOR CLARITY

Bilge pumping under way

When the crew have to sit out to keep the boat upright, they need to be able to pump water from the far bilge. One technique is to have a bilge pump located on each side, under the side-deck. From this pump the suction pipe leads to a strum box which is pulled outboard by shock-cord, or pulled further inboard by a line led to the windward side-deck. Usually the best place for the pump discharge is out through the transom.

Self-bailers

Self-bailers are fitted on many dinghies and, in spite of their disadvantages, they are well worth their cost. They are, in effect, miniature doors in the bottom of the boat which open when the boat is going fast enough so that the water in the bilge is sucked out. The suction is provided by the negative pressure under the hull and in practice this means that the self-bailer only works when the boat is going quite fast. This is of the order of 4 knots, but good bailers work even when the boat is fighting to windward, and that is when they are most needed.

Hard-up people fit one bailer the first year and, when they see just how valuable it is, they save up energetically for the second one. An 18 ft (5.5 m) boat may well have four self-bailers. Each one is fitted in a low pressure area, which is found by studying similar dinghies to see where theirs are located. There must be a trap in the floorboards by each one, as these devices should be kept hauled up and therefore sealed off until needed.

Some types are available in a cheaper version which has no guard to prevent the crew's feet from causing damage. Here, yet again, it does not pay to save money by ignoring simple safety precautions.

Transom bailers are akin to self-bailers in the bottom of the boat. They are a pair of doors, one each side of the rudder, held shut by lengths of shock cord. It is essential to maintain these bailers annually as the closing arrangements suffer from weathering. The shock-cord needs renewing roughly every twenty months when it is exposed to sunlight, and there should be a tensioning device to tighten the cord.

Transom bailers need inspecting every month. The seal, where the door abuts on the transom, needs a new rubber strip, or at least a new application of lanoline, sometimes at six-monthly intervals. The hinge, which must be on the inboard vertical edge of the door (otherwise the flap can prevent the rudder from going hard over) should be checked regularly. If it fails the door may slip sideways, in effect making a hole in the transom.

On racing dinghies these transom bailers are seldom immersed so they give little trouble. Besides, a bit of water flooding in is seldom much of a worry. Cruising boats are more heavily loaded, less carefully trimmed to keep the stern out of the water, and an accumulation of water below the floorboards is less easily noticed and more of a menace.

Sea Anchors

When wind and sea conditions get too bad for sailing the boat must be snugged down to wait till the situation improves. The ideal way to do this is to lower the mast, fit an unobtrusive tight cover over the boat and stream a sea anchor from the bow. The rudder is taken inboard or, if this is not possible, it must be swung up and the tiller lashed tightly amidships. The centreboard is hauled right up.

Sea anchors have for years been made of tough canvas in the shape of a cone, but a new type, shaped like a parachute and called after it, is coming into vogue. Whichever type is used, it must float well below the surface but not too deep. This means that there must be enough weight to ensure that it sinks, but not so much that it goes too deep or is a nuisance to carry aboard. As with most components, the sea anchor should be tried in moderate and then in increasingly severe conditions at sea, at times when it does not matter if it fails. Once it has been tried and modified as necessary it can then be carried with confidence and used when conditions are too tough for the boat with even the minimum sail set. This type of anchor can only be used when there is sea room, as the boat will slowly drift downwind. Just what the drift speed is depends on factors like windage, wind strength and the sea condition, but it must be assumed that a 1 knot drift is likely to be the minimum, so at least 25 miles of sea room are needed for each day the gale lasts.

The sea anchor is streamed from the ordinary anchor warp, but there should be a short length of chain through the fairlead at the bow. Failing this, there must be a very thick, carefully secured wrapping of cloth, or a piece of polythene tube, round the warp where it passes through the fairlead. The fairlead and mooring strong point will take a hammering so they must be much stronger than the usual toys fixed on small boat decks.

For a 16 ft (5 m) dinghy, a sea anchor about 2 ft (600 mm) across the mouth and 3 ft (900 mm) from mouth to tail, is ample. Every part must be on the massive size and there should be a tail rope 3 ft (900 mm) long with a 2 ft (600 mm) eye spliced in it, for recovering the sea anchor after use. The old idea of having a recovery line made fast to the tail and led back to the boat is no good because this line fouls the main warp by getting snarled up with it.

The cruising Laser is 16 feet long and has a tiny cuddy forward.

CHAPTER 12

Tools and Repair Materials

The tools carried will depend on the temperament of the crew and their skills. It is worth remembering that emergencies bring out hidden talents. Someone who feels that he or she has little ability to use tools may develop just enough skill on the spur of the moment. Besides, there are sometimes bystanders who are willing to help solve a problem, but they cannot do so without equipment.

As well as a knife with a shackler and spike, even a small dinghy should have screwdrivers and some form of pliers. A screwdriver to suit the fastenings on board is needed and the bigger it is, the more jobs it can cope with. For a serious cruise, a screwdriver with a blade width of ⁵⁄₁₆ in (8 mm) and another of ⅛ in (3 mm) cover most crises.

The best 'all-rounder' so far as pliers are concerned, is a 'Mole Grip'. This is a proprietary design which can be clamped onto the work piece. I used to favour the small version for dinghies, but they are less robust and more inclined to seize than the standard type which is 9 ½ in (240 mm) long. For use afloat the adjustment thread, springs, pivots and, indeed, the whole tool, apart from the outsides of the handles, should be smeared with lanoline.

'Moles' are made in England and are better than the German version which look wonderful but have a slide on one of the handles which binds and makes them difficult to use after a few weeks afloat. There is also available a simple table clamp made to hold a 'Mole' so that when the two tools are joined together the result is akin to an engineer's small vice. It is naturally important that the size of the clamp fits the 'Mole' which comes in several versions. The clamp can also be used on its own.

A small oilcan with general purpose thin oil is worth carrying on all but the smallest boats, but it must be the type which has a screw-on cap and does not spill under any circumstances.

A roll of ½ in (12 mm) wide electrician's plastic tape and a 1 in (25 mm) roll of Sylglas tape are useful. The latter is a cotton bandage thickly coated with a sticky waterproof substance. It was originally designed for sealing cracks in the glass of greenhouses, but is widely used ashore and afloat as leak-proofing in all sorts of circumstances. It is often better at stopping leaks than sticky substances in tubes, because it has the bulk and tensile strength from the cloth strip. A tube of a proprietary sealant is an asset, provided it can be used in damp conditions and provided it never goes truly hard. Those made from silicone rubber are among the best.

Only on a very extended cruise is it worth carrying epoxy resin. It needs very carefully wrapping because if it leaks out the mess is far worse than the stickiest marmalade. It is water-resistant, tacky and everlasting, and thoroughly unpleasant. It is a tremendously strong glue and the natural material for repairing fibreglass, but most versions are useless on damp surfaces, so it is seldom recommended for repairs unless the affected structure can be properly dried. It binds wood better than other glues but again, dry conditions are essential.

The ideal repair material for most jobs, ranging from a broken boom to a hole in the hull, is wood. Even dinghies used on very long trips seldom carry special pieces of ply or solid timber as mending material. Instead, the floorboards, seats, tent poles or locker fronts are pressed into service.

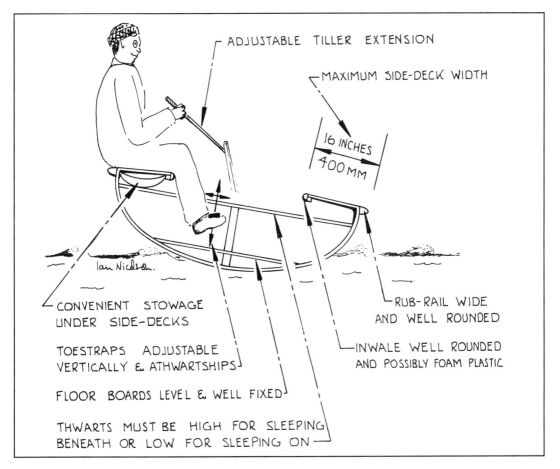

ADJUSTABLE TILLER EXTENSION

MAXIMUM SIDE-DECK WIDTH

16 INCHES
400 MM

Ian Nicolson.

CONVENIENT STOWAGE
UNDER SIDE-DECKS

TOESTRAPS ADJUSTABLE
VERTICALLY & ATHWARTSHIPS

FLOOR BOARDS LEVEL & WELL FIXED

THWARTS MUST BE HIGH FOR SLEEPING
BENEATH OR LOW FOR SLEEPING ON

RUB-RAIL WIDE
AND WELL ROUNDED

INWALE WELL ROUNDED
AND POSSIBLY FOAM PLASTIC

Sailing comfort

If the side-decks are more than the width shown, small people will not be able to get their weight right out-board. The space under the side-decks is a good place to stow gear needed when under way, such as navigation equipment, emergency items and ready use food.

Toe straps need adjusting to suit different crew, and to give a change of position on a long passage. Some boats have two sets of toe straps on each side, for gentle and maximum sitting out.

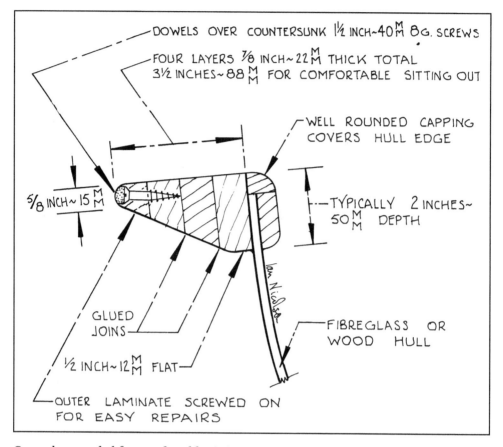

DOWELS OVER COUNTERSUNK 1½ INCH~40 M/M 8G. SCREWS

FOUR LAYERS ⅞ INCH~22 M/M THICK TOTAL
3½ INCHES~88 M/M FOR COMFORTABLE SITTING OUT

WELL ROUNDED CAPPING COVERS HULL EDGE

⅝ INCH~15 M/M

TYPICALLY 2 INCHES~ 50 M/M DEPTH

GLUED JOINS

FIBREGLASS OR WOOD HULL

½ INCH~12 M/M FLAT

OUTER LAMINATE SCREWED ON FOR EASY REPAIRS

Gunwale extended for comfortable sitting out
Many boats have narrow rub rails and gunwales, so sitting on them for long periods can be hellish. It is often easy to widen the gunwale, though it may be necessary to make an entirely new set. They can be laminated out of alternate dark and light timbers, to improve the appearance.

Screws and bolts are needed to secure wood. This means that there must be on board a hand drill with a set of metal drilling bits from about ¹⁄₁₆ in to ¼ in (1 to 6 mm) plus a countersink. The drill needs very careful protection against the damp, otherwise it will seize within a week. It should be well oiled, then wrapped in an oily rag and finally sealed with its bits (each one smeared with lanoline) in a plastic bag. If the screws are the self-tapping stainless steel kind, they can be used in wood, metal spars, fibreglass – in fact, just about everywhere.

A file, medium coarse on one side and fine on the other, would be carried on a boat making a long trip, but not otherwise. However, some form of saw is needed for even intermediate crises. The simplest is a junior hacksaw, but it is limited in the thickness through which it can cut and it is slow to use. A standard hacksaw is better, even for a week's coastal cruise. Whichever type of hacksaw is carried, there should be at least three spare blades. To quote the chandlers' favourite saying, 'More break than wear out'.

A ruler and pencil might not seem high on the priority list, but both can be part of the navigation kit, so they are well worth having. Used in conjunction with a Davies protractor a ruler is a great help on the chart. And who can navigate without three pencils – one in use, one broken and one lost in the bilge?

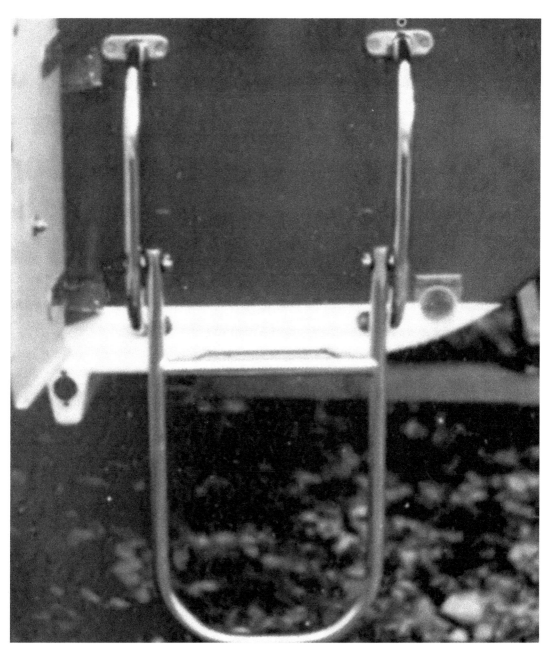

A stern boarding ladder is a great help when bathing and, if the boat capsizes, or one of the crew falls overboard, it could be a life-saver. This is the Laser 16 cruising dinghy.

With good equipment it is not hard to get a biggish boat afloat without trouble. These three photos show the launching of a Laser 16 footer off a special trailer.

CHAPTER 13

Cruising Gear

As a young apprentice naval architect I was so hard up that when I wanted to go dinghy cruising I had to make my own gear. I even borrowed charts and traced my own, to save money, and it took very many hours to make just one chart, what with all the soundings and signs.

The work I put into my gear paid off because I always made sure everything was totally reliable. Nowadays we live in a world where the accountant, not the technologist, reigns supreme. As a result, all sorts of things are made 'down to a price'. When a block disintegrates because it is slightly overloaded, we are told that it was very cheap, so reliability cannot be expected. The short answer to that is 'Nothing is cheap when the cost of failure is taken into consideration'. Gear which has no factor of safety suitable for extended cruising is not worth buying.

If in doubt, buy items which look too big, too chunky and even slightly absurd. The way to save weight is to do without things, or make each piece of equipment do two jobs.

Before buying anything, it is a good idea to talk to experienced sailing people, especially those who have been in the game for a long time. Many of them have bits and pieces off boats sold years ago which can still be used. Many a yachtsman has enough gear in the back of his car to carry out a major repair on a boat, and in his garage he has twenty times as much. I once mended an engine using a spare part which had lain under a friend's dining-room table for ten years. (Yes, his wife was delighted to get rid of it and, no, I never did discover why it had to be stowed there, but I suspect the rest of the house was chock-full of other spares).

Another source of gear, is the annual 'Boat Jumble' or sale of second-hand gear which takes place at most yachting centres. In contrast, a bad place to buy anything for a boat is a warm, well-lit indoor boat show. Here the atmosphere is too far removed from the blast of a raging gale and the tenseness of a lee shore close by, so there is too much temptation to buy what looks smart but lacks basic toughness.

Anchors

The cheapest type of anchor is the old-fashioned folding fisherman. It is reliable and works on most occasions even on uncooperative sea beds like rock, thick weed and soupy mud. Other more modern designs of anchor are good, but they tend to be at least 10 per cent more expensive, weight for weight, and it is by weight that anchors are measured. The folding fisherman has an upstanding fluke when it is dug in, so if the boat swings round on the tide, the warp may foul this projection. Sometimes the end result is that the anchor is tweaked out of the mud and the boat starts to drag.

Another worry is that in light conditions, when there is not enough wind or tide to make the boat pull her warp out straight, it is possible for the hull to settle down on top of the anchor, as the tide falls, and the boat starts to dry out. This accident can occur even if the boat does not totally dry out.

Yet another disadvantage of this anchor is that it takes a few seconds to assemble before it can be pitched overboard. When the crew have cold, wet hands, when the night is dark and the moorings are strange, those scrambled rushed seconds while one member of the crew tries to get the locking pin into the stock and the other sails the boat in zigzags to and fro, can be drama-laden.

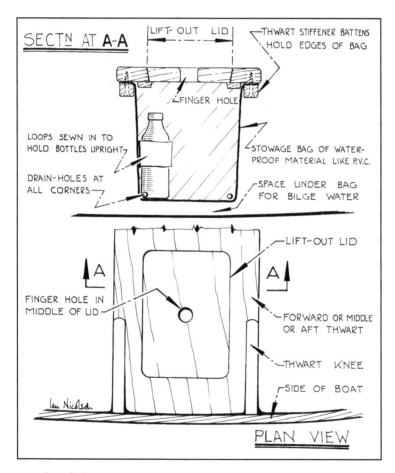

Stowage in pockets below thwarts

This type of stowage can be added to many boats. Fibreglass or wood thwarts can be modified, and the pockets may be made up by a local sailmaker. The lift-out lids should not normally be more than 12 in (300 mm) long and about 3/5 of the width of the thwart. The strength lost by cutting them out is put back by the thwart stiffeners well screwed or bolted on the underside, at the fore and aft edges.

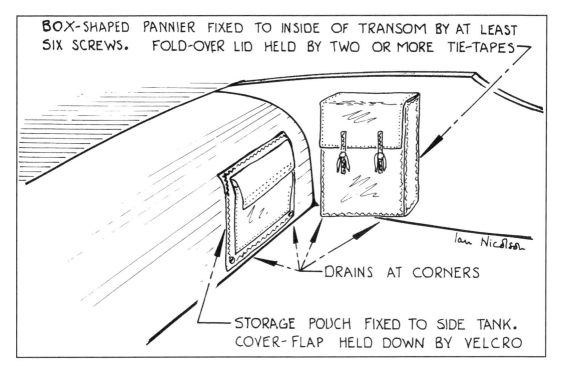

BOX-SHAPED PANNIER FIXED TO INSIDE OF TRANSOM BY AT LEAST SIX SCREWS. FOLD-OVER LID HELD BY TWO OR MORE TIE-TAPES

DRAINS AT CORNERS

STORAGE POUCH FIXED TO SIDE TANK. COVER-FLAP HELD DOWN BY VELCRO

Ian Nicolson

Cloth storage containers

These can be stitched up by a local sailmaker and are light, strong, never need painting, and come in all shapes and sizes. The lid must be secured down so that when the boat capsizes, nothing is lost. Pouches on the inboard faces of the side tanks are convenient for 'ready-use' items such as snacks, flashlights and navigation gear, yet they do not get in the way of the crew.

Bulky gear such as cookers and lanterns may have special 'cloth cupboards' made to fit exactly, but not too tightly, otherwise it will be hard to get things in and out of the containers.

This partly explains why anchors like the Danforth, CQR and Bruce are popular. The latter has no moving parts which saves pinched fingers, but it is costly. A Danforth stows flat and can be walked over, but a CQR is as unstowable as a solidified octopus. Danforths and CQRs have a good reputation for reliability and in mud the Bruce seems extremely effective.

To be reliable, an anchor has to be about 10 lb (5 kg) weight. This remark will set up a howl from anchor enthusiasts who always have some yarn about a massive boat riding out hurricanes on a tiny piece of ground tackle. However, we are interested in total and unfailing reliability, not on what has happened to one boat in one gale. For all we know, that famous anchor may have fouled a chain and so had no choice but to stay put!

For extended cruising in a boat of 16 ft (5 m) or more, it is advisable to carry a second anchor, though it is hard to find space for such a big and awkward piece of gear as ideally the second anchor should be 50 per cent heavier than the one in regular use. No one likes to lug around great lumps of unused ironware and it is true that many boats travel great distances and never need the second anchor. It is also

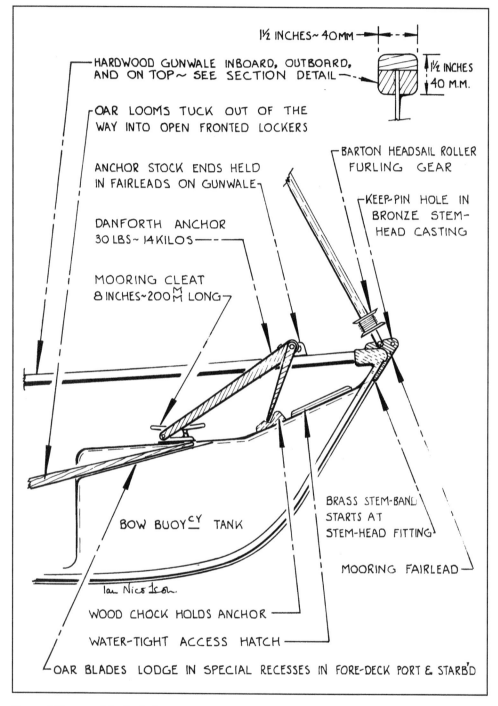

1½ INCHES~ 40MM

HARDWOOD GUNWALE INBOARD, OUTBOARD, AND ON TOP~ SEE SECTION DETAIL

1½ INCHES 40 M.M.

OAR LOOMS TUCK OUT OF THE WAY INTO OPEN FRONTED LOCKERS

BARTON HEADSAIL ROLLER FURLING GEAR

ANCHOR STOCK ENDS HELD IN FAIRLEADS ON GUNWALE

KEEP-PIN HOLE IN BRONZE STEM-HEAD CASTING

DANFORTH ANCHOR 30 LBS~ 14 KILOS

MOORING CLEAT 8 INCHES~200 M.M. LONG

BRASS STEM-BAND STARTS AT STEM-HEAD FITTING

BOW BUOY^CY TANK

MOORING FAIRLEAD

Ian Nicolson.

WOOD CHOCK HOLDS ANCHOR

WATER-TIGHT ACCESS HATCH

OAR BLADES LODGE IN SPECIAL RECESSES IN FORE-DECK PORT & STARB'D

Bow of Honnor Marine's Lugger

One of the most successful open cruising boats is the Honnor Marine Lugger which has been in production many years. It has an almost massive stem-head fitting with strong fore-and-aft fastenings through the front of the stem. The anchor is secured firmly, but handy for letting go in a hurry, and the oars are stowed in special recesses which keep them out of the way.

true that every year a few boats are lost for want of an anchor, or because the only anchor available would not hold.

An anchor's ability to grip the sea bed depends on:

1. Anchor weight.
2. Proportions.
3. The ability to dig in or hook round a rock.
4. The angle of pull of the warp.
5. The nature of the sea bed.

There is a strongly held theory that certain types of anchor simply do not dig in unless they are at least 35 lb (16 kg) weight, and, of course, when immersed the anchor in effect weighs less. This is bad news and is one reason why the traditional fisherman is so popular. No one wants to carry an anchor weighing 35 lb, even in the biggest dinghy.

The proportions of an anchor have been established by many years of trial and by scientific experiment. Anyone interested in anchor proportions – and on a dark gale-swept night one's interest can be acute – should consult *The Boat Data Book* which has scaled drawings of anchors. For details of an anchor which is easy to make see *Yacht Designer's Notebook*, published by Amberley Publishing. (Both these books are by you-know-who).

The business end of an anchor (that is the point of the fluke) should be sharp and have a fine point, like an elegant spear, so that it eases without effort into thick clay or into a heavy gravel-laden seabed. A rounded or blunt point, or a fluke which is wide and stubby, cannot be expected to dig itself into a tough seabed any better than a thick spade blade can be used for easy gardening.

Anchor Warp

On the anchor is a short length of chain and, to be safe, this should be bought from a reliable chandler. The chain can be the non-calibrated kind which has links of slightly varying size, so that they do not ride safely and smoothly over the gypsy of an anchor winch. The cash saving, as compared with the calibrated chain, is about 25 per cent. It does not pay to buy ungalvanised chain because it makes such a mess inside the boat and this mess reappears again and again, however often and quickly it is cleaned up.

The smallest chain generally available is ³⁄₁₆ in (5 mm) and ideally there should be about 16 ft (5 m). Some people, especially if inshore cruising, have half that length to save weight and money.

Another piece of chain, usually about 18 in (450 mm) may be used where the anchor warp passes over the fairlead at the bow, because there is so often dangerous wear here. If no chain is used, there must be a thick wrapping of cloth round the rope, or a length of plastic tube. Both cloth and tubing slide along the rope especially when the boat is pitching, and it is when she is jumping about that the protection is most needed. To keep the padding in place a ¹⁄₁₆ in (1 mm) line is tied to it at each end and passed through the anchor warp, or stitching is used. This means the protection is always at the same point on the warp and the whole length of the warp has to be run out to locate the padding at the fairlead.

As there will be times when a shorter length of warp has to be run out – for instance when there is not much swinging room – there must be some additional cloth on board. When this is tied in place it will need checking, especially during the first hour or two, as this is when it is likely to be forced along the warp. In an emergency two or three handkerchiefs have to be pressed into service since their total destruction is nothing compared with the cost of a chafed warp.

When it comes to deciding on the length of anchor warp it is worth looking at the chart. The rope's length has to be 6 × the depth of the water at high tide. This is so that the anchor warp makes a small angle to the sea bed surface and pulls the anchor horizontally, never upwards. Once the probable depth of water where the boat will anchor has been found, the warp's length is easily calculated. If in doubt, go for at least 100 ft (30 m) of 5/16 in (8 mm) diameter rope for serious cruising. For inshore cruising one might reduce this to ¼ in (6 mm) diameter rope, provided a lot of care is taken to avoid chafe.

In practice, it is usually possible to join the mooring warps together to form the anchor warp; the knots must be safe, but then, unlike some crews who only have racing skills, cruising people tie reliable knots in the most adverse circumstances – at night, in driving rain, after exhausting hours at sea – don't they?

Mooring Warps

The warps used for securing alongside piers and quay walls, or onto a larger yacht, will often be the same diameter as the anchor warp, or perhaps the next size down for

Built by Honnor Marine, the Drascombe Dabber is 15ft 6 inches (4.7 metres) long and has short spars which stow in the boat.

cruising in sheltered waters. Their length will be about 30 ft (10 m) and there will be at least two of them. Since for proper mooring up there must be bow and stern warps, as well as two springs, there is a need for a total of four warps. And where the rise and fall of tide is serious, say over 10 ft (3 m) the rope lengths will need doubling. It is no wonder that people cruising in a limited way in boats of the 12 ft (4 m) size, use the sheets as warps.

Fenders and Boat Rollers

Fenders are needed in great numbers for serious cruising, but for short range exploring it is tempting to save money and also to save on the amount of gear that has to be stowed away. Fenders can be made from tough canvas bags with stitched-on loops at each corner, and padding made from the crews' spare clothing inside. The clothes have to be wrapped in waterproof plastic bags, well taped up, and the canvas 'outer skin' must be doubled or trebled in thickness.

A helmsman's buoyant cushion can double as a fender and, in an emergency, a plastic water can nine-tenths full, can be pressed into service.

The smallest fenders which are sensible are about 10 in × 3 in (250 mm × 75 mm) and they should be the type with an eye at each end so that they can be hung vertically or horizontally. Four of these would be enough for careful cruising for the occasional weekend in sheltered waters. However, for serious extended cruising the minimum requirement would be six fenders 16 in × 5 in (400 mm × 125 mm) for a 16 ft (5 m) boat.

In practice, fenders are excellent extra buoyancy tanks, being soft yet tough, unlikely to puncture and extremely buoyant. Also they can be used as boat rollers when hauling the dinghy out of the water. A good case can therefore be made for having numerous fenders of the largest diameter that can be stowed on board. The Avon inflatable fender is ideal for combined buoyancy and fendering.

Best of all are 'boat rollers'. These are half cousins to fenders and buoyancy bags, being big, tough pillows, typically 16 in (400 mm) in diameter and 30 in (750 mm) long. A boat can be hauled up a beach on two, or much better four, of these, though not as easily as with a good trailer. Because rollers take a lot of punishment, they tend to deflate, so a special pump ought to be carried with them.

Knives

There was a craze for sheath knives on boats. The up-market version had a multiple sheath, with spike and a pair of pliers in separate pouches. The total weight was such that belt and even trousers sagged under the load. The manufacturers must have done a roaring trade because none of this hip-support tool chest had lanyards on, so items must have fallen overboard like confetti. The worst disadvantage of a sheath is that the whole kit has to be removed when oilskins are put on, then … what? The belt will not go on outside the oilskin jacket, and it is hardly accessible under it.

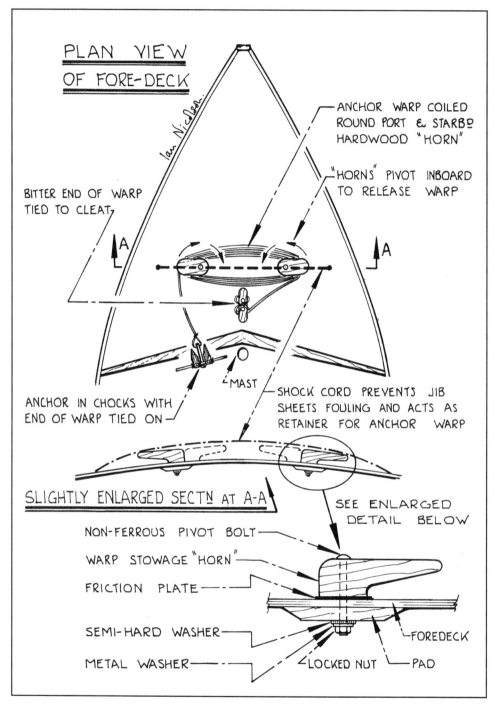

PLAN VIEW OF FORE-DECK

ANCHOR WARP COILED ROUND PORT & STARB⁰ HARDWOOD "HORN"

"HORNS" PIVOT INBOARD TO RELEASE WARP

BITTER END OF WARP TIED TO CLEAT

A   A

ANCHOR IN CHOCKS WITH END OF WARP TIED ON

MAST

SHOCK CORD PREVENTS JIB SHEETS FOULING AND ACTS AS RETAINER FOR ANCHOR WARP

SLIGHTLY ENLARGED SECTⁿ AT A-A

SEE ENLARGED DETAIL BELOW

NON-FERROUS PIVOT BOLT

WARP STOWAGE "HORN"

FRICTION PLATE

SEMI-HARD WASHER

METAL WASHER

LOCKED NUT

FOREDECK

PAD

Stowage for anchor or mooring warp

Some people keep the warp on a rotating drum, but the arrangement shown here is lighter and easier to make. Two wood horns which pivot are secured to the foredeck, and the warp is kept coiled round them. For safety there is a length of tough shock-cord over the top which is quickly pulled back and hooked over the cleat, when the warp has to be run out.

One compromise is to have the sheath fixed somewhere on the boat such as on the aft face of the main thwart, or forward face of the aft thwart, or on top of the centreboard casing, or even on the back of the mast. Provided there is some arrangement to stop the tools from falling out when the boat overturns, this arrangement has a lot to commend it. Except that, of course, the knife and then the pliers may get stolen.

On the whole, I believe that it is hard to beat the traditional stainless steel pocket knife with spike and shackler, worn on a lanyard round the neck. When the oilies are put on the knife is shifted from the trouser pocket to the oily jacket pocket. The heavy-duty type is best, and most versions need sharpening when they arrive from the makers and at monthly intervals thereafter.

Since this book was first written, many sailing people now carry a multi-tool like a Leatherman. Many of these gadgets need cleaning and the pivots need oiling every few months. A Leatherman needs a safety lanyard.

CHAPTER 14

Special Equipment

Open boat cruising is hard on gear, clothes, sleeping bags – in fact everything. So only the best made, protected by the finest materials, survives more than a few weekends afloat.

One of the best known suppliers of rugged outdoor clothing and other equipment is L. L. Bean Inc., Freeport, Maine, 04033, USA (Phone – twenty-four hours' service, 365 days per year, not an answering machine! – 1-800-221-4221 for orders and 1-800-341-4341 for customer service). Their wool shirts are warm in all conditions and smart though, of course, such shirts are always costly. Not only are Bean's clothing and sleeping bags favoured across the world, their gadgets are useful too. They sell a candle lantern which is compact and can be hung up or stood on a thwart. For a small dinghy their pocket survival tool is a multiple instrument with pliers, screwdrivers, wire-cutter, file, blade and so on. On a larger dinghy most people might favour a full set of tools.

Their space-age pens are handy as they will write in the wet and their Mag-lite flashlights are a rare breed, tough enough to stand up to outdoor conditions.

They sell transparent watertight map cases which can be used for charts. What open boat sailors particularly like is the Bean River Duffle. This is a tough, truly waterproof bag for all sorts of gear. Available in three sizes, also in blue or orange, these bags are made of PVC-coated Terylene (Dacron) and they are much stronger than polythene bags and of course, more costly too, but they are what is needed for long voyages because polythene bags seldom last long.

Anyone building or refitting a small boat for cruising needs a variety of components, many of which are not available even in a well-stocked chandlers. This is where Holt-Allen are so useful. Quite apart from a great selection of rigging and deck items, they have gadgets which are hard to find elsewhere. For instance, there is their towelling grip for tiller extensions. It is self-adhesive so anyone can put it on and enjoy the comfort and safety in all weathers.

They supply soft leather sailing gloves, though for cold conditions some people prefer wet-suit gloves. The latter do not last long when the going gets tough, whereas dinghy gloves are made to take hard use.

This firm sells a range of buoyancy bags from the large to the tiny, so that awkward corners can be filled with flotation. It is usual to have watertight built-in lockers which serve both to keep the boat afloat and to keep gear dry. But, in practice, extra buoyancy is often needed and inflatable bags are a good way of getting it inexpensively.

When sailing downwind, most cruising crews like to boom the headsail out, even if only to stop it flapping about and chafing. Holt-Allen have a selection of alloy tubes and ends so that special poles can be made up. Some people like a combined sounding pole, boathook and bearing-out pole; others like an extra strong pair of poles which can also be used as legs to keep the boat exactly upright when ashore, and so on.

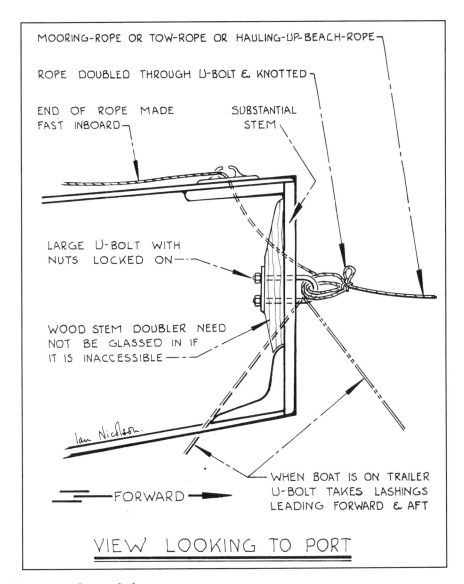

MOORING-ROPE OR TOW-ROPE OR HAULING-UP-BEACH-ROPE

ROPE DOUBLED THROUGH U-BOLT & KNOTTED

END OF ROPE MADE FAST INBOARD

SUBSTANTIAL STEM

LARGE U-BOLT WITH NUTS LOCKED ON

WOOD STEM DOUBLER NEED NOT BE GLASSED IN IF IT IS INACCESSIBLE

Ian Nicolson.

FORWARD →

WHEN BOAT IS ON TRAILER U-BOLT TAKES LASHINGS LEADING FORWARD & AFT

VIEW LOOKING TO PORT

Multi-purpose bow U-bolt

A U-bolt fitted at about half height through the stem, with a good backing block is ideal for towing, as its low location is likely to lift the bow. As an attachment point for an anchor warp or mooring it has the great advantage that the deck edge will not be chaffed. It is a good strong point for hauling the boat up a beach or lashing her to a road trailer, or to stakes in a dinghy park, to prevent gales blowing her over.

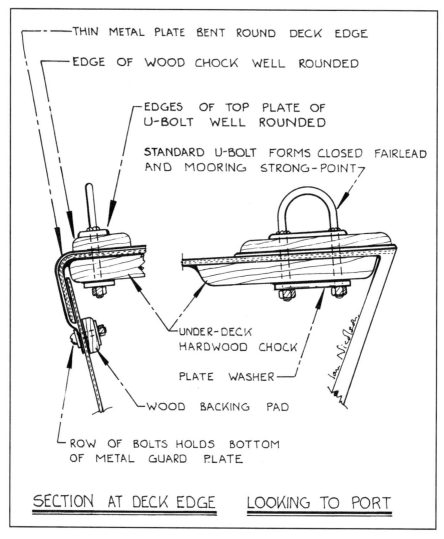

THIN METAL PLATE BENT ROUND DECK EDGE

EDGE OF WOOD CHOCK WELL ROUNDED

EDGES OF TOP PLATE OF
U-BOLT WELL ROUNDED

STANDARD U-BOLT FORMS CLOSED FAIRLEAD
AND MOORING STRONG-POINT

UNDER-DECK
HARDWOOD CHOCK

PLATE WASHER

WOOD BACKING PAD

ROW OF BOLTS HOLDS BOTTOM
OF METAL GUARD PLATE

SECTION AT DECK EDGE   LOOKING TO PORT

U-bolts have many uses

In this sketch a U-bolt is shown located right forward as an enclosed fairlead. It is hard to buy ordinary small enclosed fairleads, but the open type can be dangerous. U-bolts can also be used to hold the bottom of the forestay and headsail tack, and if strongly fitted, as a towing and mooring fitting. They are ideal for taking the lashings which hold the boat onto a trailer.

U-bolts are also good for securing the ends of personnel lifelines, and for fenders. They are far better than plain eye-bolts, and if strongly fixed they can be used to lift the boat up in a garage over winter, though for keeping it there underbody lashings are needed.

On the subject of tiller extensions, RWO sell extendable ones and also the 'ladder' type which have a row of handles at right-angles to the stem. This makes them easier to use for long periods, especially in rough conditions. Like Holt's, they also have a choice of alloy rudder heads which take lifting rudder blades. Any boat which has a fixed rudder but is to be used for general cruising, will need altering because no one wants the extra hazard of working close to the beach with a rudder which cannot be raised.

RWO supply headsail furling gear down to the size needed for small craft. The beauty of this gear is that the crew can dispose of the headsail very quickly if a squall blows up, without going forward, without wasting time uncleating a halliard and without having to lash the sail down once it has been lowered. Furlers are particularly useful when sailing single-handed or with a beginner, or in very confined waters. Their address is: RWO (Marine Equipment)Ltd, Church Road, Benfleet, Essex, SS7 4QW, England.

Holt and RWO sell all sorts of devices which make open boats safer and easier to handle. Blocks with ball bearings reduce the amount of effort needed for a job and 'muscle boxes' give extra power for tightening the headsail luff for efficient sailing, or adjusting the main outhaul to get the sail to set well. It is therefore good sense to get catalogues from these firms.

Another rare product available from Simpson-Lawrence is the Henderson Watertight Locker Door. Cheap, light versions of this access hatch for watertight lockers are available from dinghy chandlers, but for cruising the heavier Henderson version is what is needed. It has been approved for use on lifeboats, which indicates its level of seaworthiness. The access hole through this 'door' is just over 7 in (175 mm) diameter, so clever owners make all their gear small enough to fit through this size of circle.

CHAPTER 15

The Home Base

When not in use, a boat needs a comfortable home just as much as her owner. Unless there are good working conditions where the boat is kept the annual refit and the maintenance will be less than excellent. The cruises will be less safe, less easy and certainly less fun if the boat is not at her peak of condition when she sets out.

The home base ideally should be within a short walk of the owner's home and, best of all, should be connected to his house so that he can reach his boat without going out into bad weather. This will mean that any spare moment he has, he will spend adjusting, cleaning, rubbing down, painting, greasing, trimming ... the list is endless as any boat owner knows.

The ideal home for a boat is a dry shed or warehouse, empty bedroom, or even a garage, provided it does not have oil on the floor. If the boat is kept at a boatyard shed, try and find that rare corner where there are no roof leaks. Ideally, there should be 6 ft (2 m) of clear space all round the boat. If that is impossible, the boat should be on some sort of mobile cradle or trailer which allows her to be moved easily within the available space so that she can be worked upon port or starboard, at bow or stern.

The boat store should be vandal-proof, which nowadays calls for precautions which are numerous.

The Essentials

Working on a boat requires plenty of light. Much of the time spent on maintenance is usually during weekday evenings, so plenty of artificial light is essential. In addition there must be four electric sockets; two are the working pair, for a wandering light and electric drill or sander, one is for the heater and one for brewing coffee.

Experienced boat owners will know that there is no such thing as a sufficiency of electric power sources and will have a multi-socket plug box as well. Where there is no electrical supply, a pair of paraffin (kerosene) pressure lanterns are needed. They must be the pressure type; the ordinary hurricane lights only give out glow-worm glimmers. Alternatively, get a pair of the modern portable gas lanterns with incandescent mantles. As the lanterns may also be used when cruising, the type selected should be able to stand up to rain and spray. Only those with lamp glasses which can withstand wetting when hot are any good.

The most important piece of furniture is the work bench with vice or, better still, with both a carpenter's vice and an engineer's vice. Failing this, at least have a 'Workmate' ... one of those folding portable tables which incorporates a vice with bench stops and a step. The operator jams one foot down on the step to keep the whole affair firmly on the ground. In practice, when using one of these excellent but rather light work tables, it is best to fix it to the ground rigidly.

A supply of water is handy but not essential. For some people, a nearby source of cooked meals is an asset.

Above all, the access to the boat's home must be reasonable. My design office was 'launched' by building its first boat two stories up, in the middle of a city.

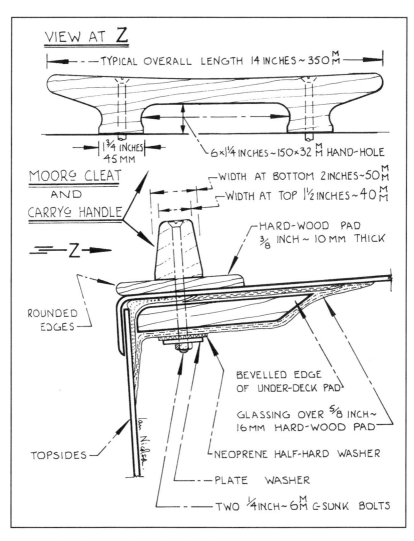

VIEW AT Z

TYPICAL OVERALL LENGTH 14 INCHES ~ 350 MM

1¾ INCHES 45 MM

6 × 1¼ INCHES ~ 150 × 32 MM HAND-HOLE

MOORG CLEAT AND CARRYG HANDLE

WIDTH AT BOTTOM 2 INCHES ~ 50 MM

WIDTH AT TOP 1½ INCHES ~ 40 MM

HARD-WOOD PAD ⅜ INCH ~ 10 MM THICK

Z

ROUNDED EDGES

BEVELLED EDGE OF UNDER-DECK PAD

GLASSING OVER ⅝ INCH ~ 16 MM HARD-WOOD PAD

TOPSIDES

NEOPRENE HALF-HARD WASHER

PLATE WASHER

TWO ¼ INCH ~ 6 MM G-SUNK BOLTS

Combined mooring cleat and carrying handle

It is often better to fix a mooring cleat at the edge of the foredeck, rather than in the middle. The side of the deck is stronger, and close to the topsides, so even in extreme conditions, there is less likelihood of the cleat or adjacent deck being torn out.

The size of the hand-hole cannot be reduced even on a very small boat and, in any case, even on little boats, large cleats are practical and reassuring in rough weather.

To get the boat to the water the 18 ft (5.5 m) hull had to be eased through the aperture left after a massive window had been carefully taken out. This was many years ago in the days before mobile cranes, so the operation took a long time, much rigging of tackle onto trees and roof edges and also more patience than people have these days.

It is better to find somewhere accessible by lorry or road trailer. Ideally, there should be ample floor space, because boats suspended high up under roof beams get less than their fair share of loving care. However, it is better to keep the craft under cover away up under a roof than out in the open, exposed to the weather.

Any boat needs four suspension points or keel chocks. Though there is a fashion for leaving boats for long periods supported only at two points, this is poor practice and every experienced surveyor has tales to tell of hulls suffering from subtle distortions.

The best kept boats tend to be mollycoddled. They may be in dark, dingy, disused factories, or in some corner of a typical boatyard ... a place which seldom gets tidied, cleaned, or maintained. Under those conditions, the sensible owner surrounds his boat with a tent of polythene sheet, especially if there is a risk that she will suffer from roof leaks. The top of the tent slopes steeply to deflect falling drips. Outside the entrance to this tent there is a large doormat so that even the most insensitive visitor wipes his feet. Inside there may well be an old carpet under the boat and just inside the door there will be another doormat to drive home the importance of keeping the whole area clean.

Adjacent locked cupboards for the boat's gear are useful, but most people like to take equipment home so that they can work on it during the off season. Certainly less robust items such as echo-sounders and flashlights are best kept at home.

Much the best way to work on the bottom of any boat is 'downhand', that is with the job below the person doing it. Lying under a boat, working upwards, is so tiring and awkward that even experts only do moderately well. So, the ideal storage place has arrangements for turning the boat over.

If there are no overhead beams which can support a batch of tackles, there should be space all round for lots of people to gather, for lifting and turning the boat. When the shed is small, but has large end doors, it is sometimes good policy to open these doors wide, jam them firmly, then rig tarpaulins over them, so as to extend the length of the shed. In this way a 16 ft shed can house a 15 ft boat and still have working space at each end.

If a boat has to be stored in the open it is often worth doing this in a boatyard. At the first sign of spring one or two yachts will be moved out of the storage shed to go afloat and the owner of an open boat can then push his craft into the newly available space and have the advantages of working under cover.

In some boat sheds there is room between the big yachts which are laid up, especially if they are deep-keeled sailing yachts. But beware of enthusiastic amateurs applying antifouling paint; they tend to splash it around and I've even seen them get it splattered onto their own cars!

When budgeting for a year's sailing, the cost of the winter storage has to be remembered. Because open boats are so easy to transport on road trailers or on top of cars, it is often cheaper to keep the boat inland rather than in a boatyard. However, many yards have all sorts of useful facilities such as chandlery departments, lifting tackle, and other owners with special tools which can be borrowed.

Running Rigging Sizes

As small ropes are hard to handle, some of these dimensions are well over the requirements for adequate strength. Likewise, these sizes can be used for smaller dinghies without being too massive because they will be big enough to give a good grip even in cold and wet conditions.

	Rope Diameter		Sheave Diameter		Min. Sheave Diameter	
	in	mm	in	mm	in	mm
For dinghies around 14–16 ft (4.2–5 m)						
Halliards	¼	6.5	1 ¾	45	1	25
Topping lift	³⁄₁₆	5	1 ½	40	1	25
Burgee halliard	¹⁄₁₆	2	1	25	⅝	15
Main and jib sheets	⁷⁄₁₆	11	2 ½	65	1 ¾	45
Spinnaker sheets	³⁄₁₆	5	1 ½	40	1	25
For dinghies about 18–20 ft (5.5–6 m)						
Halliards	⁵⁄₁₆	8	2	50	1 ⅛	30
Topping lift	¼	6.5	1 ¾	45	1	25
Burgee halliard	⅛	3	1	25	⅝	15
Main and jib sheets	⁷⁄₁₆	11	2 ½	65	1 ¾	45
Spinnaker sheets	¼	6.5	1 ¾	45	1	25

The Ian Nicolson Trilogy

Ian Nicolson

In this trilogy, Ian Nicolson tells the fascinating tales of his
adventures with yachts on both sides of the Atlantic.

978 1 4456 5196 5

352 pages

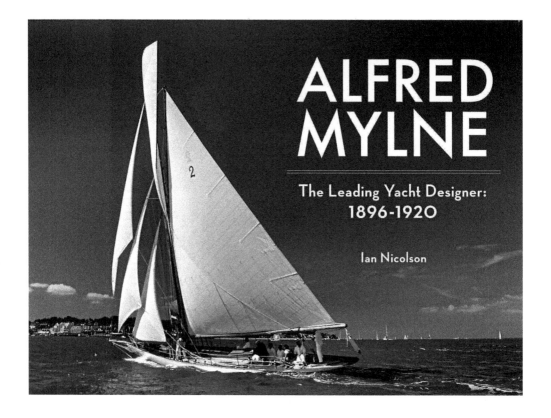

Alfred Mylne: The Leading Yacht Designer
1896–1920

Ian Nicolson

In this book, Ian Nicolson uses original plans from the archives
of Alfred Mylne to demonstrate the beauty of the earliest Mylne
designs and to tell the story of Alfred Mylne the man.

978 1 4456 4633 6

160 pages, illustrated

Yacht Designer's Notebook

Ian Nicolson

This fully revised third edition of a classic manual is a mine of
information for yachtsmen to customise their boats.

978 1 4456 5158 3

192 pages, illustrated throughout

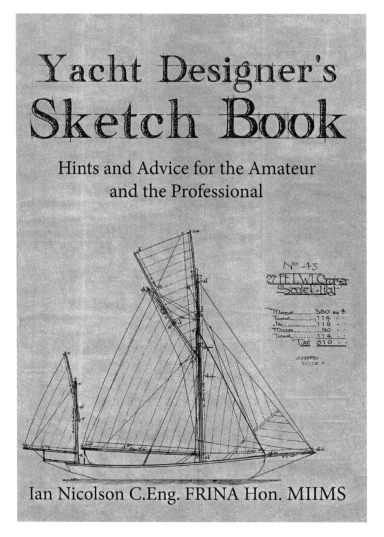

Yacht Designer's Sketch Book

Ian Nicolson

Ian Nicolson provides a wide range of easy-to-follow designs for the owner, user, builder or repairer of any yacht or small boat.

978 1 4456 5150 7

160 pages, illustrated throughout

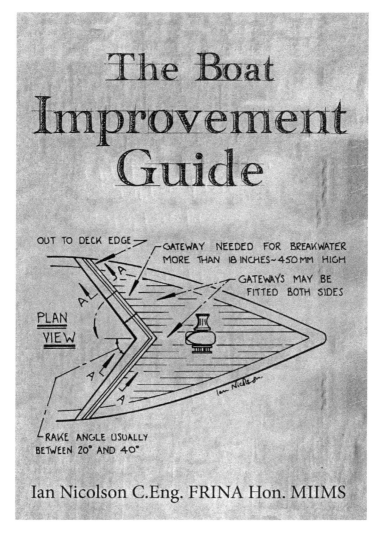

The Boat Improvement Guide

Ian Nicolson

Ian Nicolson provides handy tips for improving your boat.

978 1 4456 5331 0

160 pages, illustrated throughout

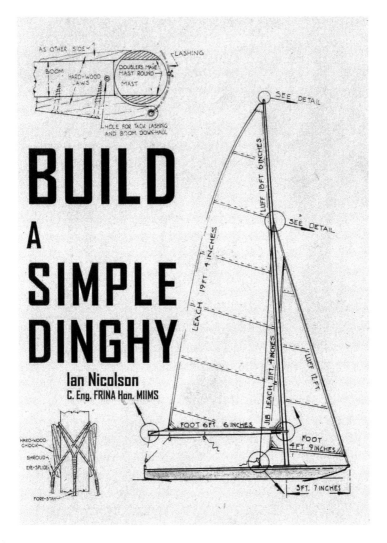

Build a Simple Dinghy

Ian Nicolson

A guide with enough information on how to build these boats and
some plans are available at low cost.

978 1 4456 5354 5

96 pages, illustrated throughout

Available from all good bookshops or order direct
from our website www.amberley-books.com

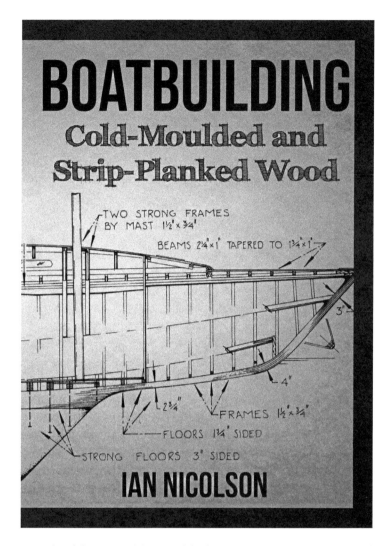

Boatbuilding: Cold-Moulded and Strip-Planked Wood

Ian Nicolson

This book is a practical guide to both methods, starting from the design requirements, necessary tools and working conditions, and choice of timber through step-by-step construction and repair.

978 1 4456 5166 8

192 pages, illustrated throughout

Available from all good bookshops or order direct
from our website www.amberley-books.com